# THE BOSTON MOB GUIDE

# THE BOSTON MOB GUIDE

## Hit Men, Hoodlums & Hideouts

# Beverly Ford & Stephanie Schorow

Charleston      London

THE
History
PRESS

Published by The History Press
Charleston, SC  29403
www.historypress.net

*Cover photos courtesy of the Boston Public Library, Print Department and the Leslie Jones Collection.*

First published 2011
Second printing 2012
Third printing 2012

Manufactured in the United States

ISBN 978.1.60949.420.9

Library of Congress Cataloging-in-Publication Data
Ford, Beverly.
The Boston mob guide : hit men, hoodlums and hideouts / Beverly Ford and Stephanie
Schorow.
p. cm.
ISBN 978-1-60949-420-9
1. Organized crime--Massachusetts--Boston. 2. Gangsters--Massachusetts--Boston. 3.
Criminals--Massachusetts--Boston.  I. Schorow, Stephanie. II. Title.
HV6452.M4F67 2011
364.10609744'61--dc23
2011037866

# CONTENTS

Acknowledgements 7

Introduction 9

1. All Roads Lead to Whitey 13

2. The Men in the Mob 25

3. Hangouts and Hideouts 93

4. Hits and Heists 109

5. Tinsel Townies: Boston Mobsters in the Movies 137

Afterword 149

Sources 151

Index 153

About the Authors 159

# ACKNOWLEDGEMENTS

The authors would like to thank the extraordinary staff of the Boston Public Library for their generous help in locating photos and other materials for this project, as well as former *Boston Herald* photographer and investigator John Landers. The authors would also like to thank Jeff Saraceno at The History Press for "making us an offer we couldn't refuse" and his patience during the process of putting this book together.

# INTRODUCTION

On June 22, 2011, the game of "Where's Whitey?" ended forever. After sixteen years on the lam, Boston's most notorious gangster, James J. "Whitey" Bulger, was captured without incident in Santa Monica, California. The day that many Bostonians thought would never come had arrived, closing an infamous chapter in the city's history.

The twists and turns of Whitey's long criminal record—a tale so filled with double-crosses, ironic shifts and colorful characters that it reads like fiction—was a fitting climax to Boston's long relationship with the dark side. Along with revolutionaries, statesmen, philosophers and authors, Boston has seen a colorful cadre of wise guys, bad boys, criminal masterminds and low-life hoods who have left their mark on the City on the Hill. The book that you now hold in your hand is a guide to these characters and the places they once walked and ruled with intimidation, fear and violence.

And what a crew they are! Anyone not living under a rock in the past year knows that Whitey Bulger was captured, but not everyone knows the full extent of his sordid yet mesmerizing saga, not even longtime Bostonians. Many have heard of Stephen "the Rifleman" Flemmi, Francis "Cadillac Frank" Salemme or Joe "the Animal" Barboza; many don't know how they got their nicknames or how they are interconnected. And then there are hoodlums whose names are only dimly remembered—men like Steve Wallace and "Dodo" Walsh of the Gustin gang in South Boston, Joseph Lombardo of the North End or Charles "King" Solomon, who once presided over the Cocoanut Grove nightclub. There are the Italians: Gennaro Angiulo and

This was the photo flashed around the world in June 2011 when fugitive James "Whitey" Bulger was arrested at an apartment in Santa Monica, California, where he had been living under the name of "Charles Gasko." *FBI file photo.*

his brothers and the Rhode Island–based Patriarca family; the Irish: Buddy McLean and Howie Winter of Somerville; as well as representatives of other immigrant groups and ethnicities. Often, there has been a thin line between legal and illegal businesses. It was not unusual to find Boston families in which one son was a cop and another was a bootlegger, one was a lawyer and the other a thug. Whitey Bulger and his brother, the former Massachusetts senate president William "Billy" Bulger, are prime examples.

In doing their research, both authors were repeatedly struck by the complicated but strong connections among the various mobsters. Bev, an investigative reporter, had to untangle numerous threads in Whitey's world, a tough challenge even though she had covered the gangster for years as a cop beat reporter for the *Boston Herald*. Stephanie found that the names she had encountered while researching the 1942 Cocoanut Grove nightclub and the 1950 Brink's robbery for her previous books popped up again in the 1950s, 1960s and 1970s. Boston, at its core, is a small town, and the strong connections that once linked Brahmin bluebloods and the literary elite are eerily mirrored by the ties among the hit men, loansharks, guns-for-hire and dope dealers who also walked Boston's streets.

It's hard to keep track of them all. There are many good books out there on Boston's mob landscape; we know—we've read a lot of them (see the bibliography), and we relied on the work done over the past fifty years by the ink-stained scribes of the *Boston Globe* and the *Boston Herald*, as well as newspapers long gone, such as the *Record American*. Moreover, not a few of the mobsters mentioned here have published their own memoirs, adding their own perspectives on events. You can read this book on its own or you can refer to it when you read the others; we intend it to be the scorecard to use while getting to know the players.

Because it gets complicated very quickly. There's the Prohibition period, with bootlegging by Russian Jewish mobster Charles "King" Solomon and perhaps—as it has been alleged—by the patriarch of the Kennedy clan,

Joseph Kennedy. Early Irish gangsters are represented by the South Boston–based Gustin Gang, which ran afoul of the North End Italian mobsters headed by Joseph Lombardo. In the 1950s, the Winter Hill Gang, based in Somerville, emerged, led by, in succession, Buddy McLean, Howie Winter and Bulger. Then there are the battles between the Mullen Gang and the Killeens of South Boston and, in the 1960s, a full-scale mob war among factions from Charlestown, South Boston and Somerville. It's a dizzying series of hits, revenge slayings and tenuous alliances that are both fascinating and horrifying. Add in the operations of the New England Mafia—the Angiulos of the North End and the Patriarcas of Rhode Island—and you have a thick, uneasy stew of connections, partnerships and animosities. Finally, there's Whitey, who has connections to nearly all the players here, either as a sometimes partner or deadly rival. Whether you're new to Boston or have grown up here, *Boston Mob Guide: Hit Men, Hoodlums and Hideouts* will fill you in on the essentials: what you know, what you don't know and what you think you know. No one volume could possibly cover every figure—much less every hit—in Boston's organized crime, but we believe this book is a fair sampling of mob history.

This book was written after we received an offer we couldn't refuse: The History Press asked us to write a guide to Boston's gangsters and their hangouts and hits. (At first, the editors wanted a guide to Boston's "mafia," and we had to explain that crime was an equal opportunity employer here for the Irish, Italian, Jews and Chinese.) Because Boston is such a compact city, mobster haunts and hideouts are cheek-by-jowl with other hallmarks of history. Just a stone's throw from the Old North Church, famed for its one-if-by-land, two-if-by-sea message to Paul Revere, was the Prince Street headquarters of the Angiulo gang. Right on the vaunted Freedom Trail is the North Terminal Garage, the site of the infamous Brink's heist in 1950. The spectacular ocean views afforded on a walk around Castle Island in South Boston are enjoyed by hundreds of people daily and were once the backdrop for conversations by a strolling Whitey Bulger and his lieutenants, Kevin Weeks and Steve "The Rifleman" Flemmi. A couple blocks from the hustle of Downtown Crossing is the site of the Blackfriars club, in which five people, including a prominent TV reporter, died in a hail of bullets in 1978 in a case that remains unsolved. Many of the movies about Boston's bad guys were filmed on location, and in the last chapter, we find the spots where Tinsel Town met The Town.

This book is organized into five chapters. In Chapter 1, we delve into the life of Whitey Bulger. In Chapter 2, we profile the most prominent of the area's hoodlums. In Chapter 3, we look at local hangouts and hideouts. In Chapter 4, we detail some of the most notorious gangland hits or murders. And in Chapter 5, we look at the Boston mob in the movies.

While we abhor the violence and sorrow these hoodlums brought to their victims, their victims' families and the city itself, there is an undeniable fascination with how they operated on the far side of the law. Worldwide attention to Bulger's arrest, which came during our research, only underscores the dark allure. Every city has its underbelly, the dark corners where naughty meets noir, where the law is a moveable feast, not a line in the sand. Few places have an underbelly as colorful—and tragic—as the mean streets of Boston.

## Chapter 1
# ALL ROADS LEAD TO WHITEY

JAMES BULGER
*Nickname: "Whitey"*
*Addresses: 327 West Fourth Street, South Boston;*
*1012 Third Street, Santa Monica, California*
*Aliases: Thomas F. Baxter, Tom Harris, Tom Bulger, Mark Shapeton,*
*Thomas Marshall, Charles Gasko*
*Born: September 3, 1929, Dorchester, Massachusetts*
*Association: Winter Hill Gang*

The name has been flashed around the country, but just who is James "Whitey" Bulger? Even before his sensational capture in 2011, his name was legendary both in organized crime circles and on the streets of his hometown, although not quite for the same reason.

To some, James "Whitey" Bulger was a heartless thug who killed for pleasure. To others, he seemed a beneficent Robin Hood, stealing from the rich, protecting the poor and keeping his South Boston neighborhood free from drugs. To his family, he was the brother of Senator William "Billy" Bulger, one of the most powerful politicians in Massachusetts history. Whoever he was, James "Whitey" Bulger was also, at one point, the most wanted man in America, a title he shared with Osama bin Laden, the mastermind behind the September 11, 2001 attacks on the United States.

The road from small-time hoodlum to the FBI's most wanted was a long one, littered with bodies, payoffs, greed and corruption. It would end,

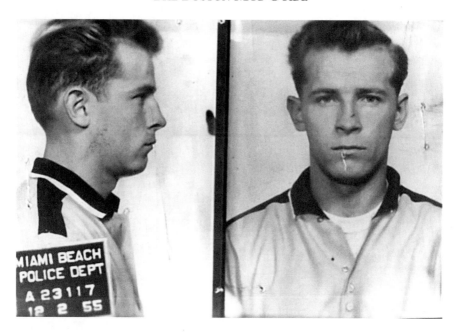

A mug shot of Whitey Bulger from 1955. *Courtesy of the Boston Public Library, Print Department.*

however, on June 22, 2011, in the beachfront community of Santa Monica, California, with the arrest of a frail and elderly Bulger sixteen years after he went on the lam. Bulger had been running from the law all his life, and good luck—and friends in high places—helped him evade arrest for decades.

From the beginning, Bulger's life seemed less than charmed. Born to James Joseph Bulger Sr. and Jane McCarthy Bulger on September 3, 1929, in Dorchester, Massachusetts, he was the oldest of six children in a household struggling to make a life in post-Depression Boston. His father, a union laborer and sometimes longshoreman who occasionally worked as a clerk at the Charlestown Navy Yard, lost his arm in an industrial accident when his son was still a boy, sending the family into a spiral of poverty. When he was about nine years old, Bulger's parents moved the family from the North End into a three-bedroom apartment on Logan Way in the Mary Ellen McCormick Housing Project, a series of brick tenements on the fringes of South Boston, also known as Southie (which is not to be confused with Boston's South End). The family's apartment was located just a short distance from Castle Island, a crescent-shaped stretch of beaches and walkways along Boston Harbor that would become one of Bulger's favorite haunts. In the years to come, he would be photographed there many times by undercover investigators as he walked with mob associates.

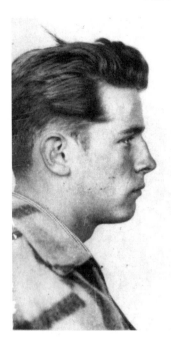

A classic mug shot of Whitey Bulger from 1953. *Courtesy of the Boston Police Department.*

Yet it was a friendship made on the rough-and-tumble streets of South Boston that would forever change the course of Bulger's life and the lives of many others. It was here that Bulger met John Connolly, a Southie neighbor eleven years his junior who would eventually become his FBI handler. Connolly lived on O'Callahan Way in the Old Colony Housing project and, later, at the Harbor Point Housing project, a short distance away, and his family worshiped at nearby St. Monica's Church, which the Bulgers also attended.

Whether fact or folklore, Connolly often told a story about how Bulger walked into an ice cream parlor where three eight-year-olds, including a young Connolly, were standing at the counter. Perhaps overcome by generosity, Bulger offered to buy the youngsters each an ice cream cone. Connolly, however, balked, saying that his parents told him never to accept gifts from strangers. According to Connolly, Bulger picked him up, sat him on the counter and said, "Hey kid, I'm no stranger. Your mother and father are from Ireland. My mother and father are from Ireland. What kind of ice cream do you want?" Reassured, Connolly replied, "Vanilla."

As an FBI agent in Boston, Connolly would cite that story as the beginning of his long friendship with the South Boston crime kingpin. It was an admiration that would lead Bulger's handler down a precipitous path into prison. Yet as a

The Old Colony Housing Development, near where James "Whitey" Bulger and his brother, the former Massachusetts Senate president, William Bulger, grew up and hung out. This was one of the public housing apartment complexes known as the "Southie Projects," where generations of Boston's Irish lived until court-ordered school desegregation in the 1970s brought a mix of ethnicities into South Boston. *Photo by Stephanie Schorow.*

young boy, Connolly looked to Bulger as a childhood hero whose antics, even as a fourteen-year-old, were already drawing the attention of law enforcement. By that age, already a member of a street gang known as the Shamrocks, Bulger was facing a larceny rap. Later charges of robbery, along with assault and battery, helped earn him a stint in a juvenile reformatory.

In their book, *Black Mass*, authors Dick Lehr and Gerard O'Neill portray the young mobster as a smart but lazy student who preferred street fighting and car chases to studying. Unlike his brother Billy, who was four years younger and a solid student, Bulger hated school and dropped out before he could graduate from high school. He also hated to be called "Whitey," a nickname earned—and despised—because of his blond hair. Instead, he asked people to call him Jim.

By 1948, fresh out of reform school, Bulger joined the United States Air Force, where he spent more than his share of time in the brig. Despite those lockups, and even though he was arrested in 1950 for being AWOL, he returned to Massachusetts in 1952 with an honorable discharge.

Back in the old neighborhood, Bulger returned to what he knew best—stealing. Before long, he was back under arrest for a string of bank robberies and truck hijackings in Massachusetts, Rhode Island and Indiana. Nabbed on those charges at a Revere, Massachusetts nightclub in 1956, police noticed that his blond hair was dyed black. It wouldn't be the last time investigators would hear about the chameleon-like Bulger dressing in disguise.

While in federal custody for those crimes in Atlanta, Georgia, Bulger, hoping to reduce his sentence, volunteered to participate in trials of a new drug, lysergic acid diethylamide, more commonly known by its street name: LSD. "We were given the LSD in varying dosages—some times light some times massive—that would plunge us into the depths of insanity and followed by periods of deep depression, suicidal thought and nightmares and interrupted sleep," Bulger would later write, according to *Boston Herald* columnist, author and radio talk show host Howie Carr. Bulger and six other inmates were recruited for the project "by lies and deception…encouraged

to be human guinea pigs in a noble humanitarian cause—searching for a cure for schizophrenia," Bulger wrote in his perfect penmanship. As a result of those experiments, Bulger claimed that he suffered frequent bouts of insomnia and nightmares.

In November 1959, he was transferred to Alcatraz, the maximum-security prison in San Francisco Bay, after guards suspected he was planning to escape. Confined to solitary confinement on several occasions because he defied guards' orders, Bulger was moved to Leavenworth Federal Penitentiary in Kansas in 1962 when Alcatraz closed. Seven months later, he was moved again, this time to Lewisburg Federal Penitentiary in Pennsylvania, from which he was released in 1965 after serving nine years in prison.

While James "Whitey" Bulger was descending deeper into criminal life, his brother, William Bulger, was a rising star on the Boston political scene. As a state representative and later state senator and president of the senate, Billy Bulger became a political force to be reckoned with. Just how much sibling rivalry drove the lives of the two South Boston boys is an issue for the friends of Dr. Freud. *Courtesy of the Boston Public Library, Print Department.*

By the time he returned to his home in South Boston, Bulger's younger brother, William, was making a name for himself as a member of the Massachusetts House of Representatives, where he served four terms. William Bulger would later move on to become state senator, and after nearly two decades as the iron-willed president of the Massachusetts Senate, he was named president of the University of Massachusetts. He resigned from that post in 2003 under pressure by then Massachusetts governor Mitt Romney after he refused to cooperate with investigators searching for his brother.

As ambitious as his younger brother, Whitey Bulger also had plans for advancement, albeit of a different kind. He hooked up with Donald Killeen—the leader of an Irish organized crime gang in South Boston—and, by 1971, became involved in a mob war with a rival Irish gang, the Mullen Gang. The gun battles between the two groups left bullet-riddled bodies across the state.

Kevin Weeks, a Bulger pal and fellow hoodlum, recalled how during the height of the mob war, Bulger mistakenly killed the wrong man after stopping the driver of a car in South Boston. "Jimmy was driving down Seventh Street in South Boston when he saw Paulie [Paul McGonagle] driving toward him," Weeks recalled in his 2006 book, *Brutal: The Untold Story of My Life Inside Whitey Bulger's Irish Mob.* "Jimmy pulled up beside him, window to window, nose to nose, and called his name. As Paulie looked over, Jimmy shot him right between the eyes. Only at that moment, just as he pulled the trigger, Jimmy realized it wasn't Paulie. It was Donald, the most likable of the McGonagle brothers, the only one who wasn't involved in anything."

Bulger rushed to Dorchester to tell his mentor, Billy O'Sullivan, about the mistake. O'Sullivan, who was cooking, looked up from the stove and calmly told Bulger not to worry. "He wasn't healthy anyway. He smoked. He would have gotten lung cancer," Weeks remembered O'Sullivan saying. Then, turning back to his cooking, he quietly asked Bulger, "How do you want your pork chops?"

Not long afterward, O'Sullivan become another victim of the Irish mob wars, killed when he was ambushed by Paul McGonagle, Bulger's intended target and twin brother to Donald McGonagle. Bulger would later take out Paul McGongagle. It would be twenty-five years before his body and the bodies of two other Bulger murder victims would be dug up on Tenean Beach in Dorchester.

Perhaps realizing that he was outmaneuvered and outgunned by the Mullen Gang, Bulger is said to have secretly approached Howie Winter, head of Somerville's Winter Hill Gang, with an offer. He would end the turf

Tenean Beach in Dorchester, with a colorful Boston Gas storage tank in the background. To the right is the skyline of Boston's Financial District. Three of Whitey's victims ended up buried here. *Photo by Beverly Ford.*

battle by killing the leaders of the rival Killeen Gang, then the dominant gang in South Boston. It wasn't long before Donald Killeen was shot to death outside his home in Framingham, about thirty miles west of Boston. His death provided an opportunity to merge the two Irish factions, with Winter as head of both. In a touch of irony, Bulger would later take as his mistress Catherine Greig, the ex-wife of Robert McGonagle, the brother of twins Donald and Paul McGonagle whose early deaths Bulger had hastened.

By the 1970s, with his Irish competition out of the picture, Bulger was in solid with Howie Winter and his Winter Hill Gang, whose membership included an old friend, Stephen Flemmi. Soon, he and Flemmi were working as enforcers for Winter, effectively collecting on debts with a fierceness that put other gangsters to shame.

The gang's big money, however, came from fixing horse races by paying off jockeys. At racetracks up and down the Atlantic seaboard, the fix was in. Then a jockey from Atlantic City stepped forward and became a federal snitch. Caught up in that investigation was "Fat Tony" Ciulla, Winter's main race fixer. With a sentence of four to six years hanging over his head, Ciulla soon started talking, promising to testify against the Winter Hill Gang if the authorities would put him in the federal Witness Protection Program. Among those he later identified as being part of the race-fixing scheme were Bulger, Flemmi and Winter.

When indictments in the case were returned in 1979, however, neither Bulger nor Flemmi was charged. Twenty-one other people, including mob hit man John Martorano, were among those indicted. By now, Bulger and Flemmi had both become valuable informants for the FBI. Connolly, now working as a special agent with the bureau, and his supervisor, John Morris, wanted to bring down Boston's Italian mob, and they needed Bulger and Flemmi's help. Soon, Connolly and other agents were meeting with the two mobsters on a regular basis, having dinner with them and exchanging gifts on special occasions. The agents leaked information to the pair as well, informing them of law enforcement investigations and warning them of pending indictments. Their friendship, it seems, became more than that of informant and handler.

Bulger didn't like the idea of becoming a government snitch, even though he had traded information with the FBI since 1975, just a few years after his pal Flemmi signed on as an informant with the feds. Connolly was persuasive. He convinced Bulger that investigators would leave him and Flemmi alone if they promised to help take down the Italian mob. In 1980, Flemmi and Bulger supplied the FBI with a layout of the 98 Prince Street office of mob underboss Gennaro Angiulo, leading agents to plant electronic listening devices that would crack open their investigation into the Boston Mafia.

With Somerville gangster Howie Winter indicted on charges of fixing horse races and his Italian rivals soon facing indictments of their own, Bulger was poised to take over Boston's organized crime contingent. Now in a leadership position in the Winter Hill Gang, he soon relocated the gang's headquarters from Marshall Motors in Somerville, Massachusetts, to Lancaster Foreign Car Service, a garage on Lancaster Street not far from the Boston Garden, home to the Boston Celtics basketball team and the Boston Bruins hockey team. When state police investigators, noticing a number of bookies coming and going from the garage, got a warrant to bug the property, something odd happened. Their electronic listening devices never picked up anything incriminating. It would be years later before the investigating troopers would learn that Bulger had been tipped off to their probe by his pals at the FBI.

Knowing his federal contacts would protect him emboldened the mob kingpin. Soon, Bulger was carrying out hits with little fear of retribution. Among those killed was a bookie named Louis Latif, who made the worst decision of his life one night in 1980 when he stopped by Triple O's bar, a notorious South Boston mob hangout, to talk with Bulger about some missing bookkeeping money that Bulger suspected Latif was using to buy cocaine. Even worse, Latif was refusing to pay Bulger a cut of his trafficking profits and had murdered two people without Bulger's permission. It wasn't long before Latif's dead body was wrapped in plastic, hauled out the back

State Senator Joe Moakley and a young State Representative William Bulger, chair and vice-chair, respectively, of a legislative committee on—irony of ironies—crime and violence in this telling photo from 1967. By this time, Billy Bulger's brother Whitey had a long and growing rap sheet. *Courtesy of the Boston Public Library, Print Department.*

door and placed in the trunk of a car, only to be discovered days later at another location.

One month after that murder, on May 27, 1981, Roger Wheeler, the owner of World Jai Alai, was shot to death in the parking lot of a country club in Tulsa, Oklahoma—another Bulger casualty. Wheeler suspected the Winter Hill boys were skimming profits from his Jai Alai operation in Connecticut, and he was threatening to go to authorities. Instead, Bulger hired Winter Hill executioner John Martorano to make sure Wheeler was silenced. Wearing a fake beard and clutching a handgun inside a brown paper bag, Martorano calmly walked up to his victim's car and shot Wheeler between the eyes.

Just fifteen months after Wheeler's death, another World Jai Alai official turned up dead, the victim of a nervous mobster worried he was about to flip and tell prosecutors about the skimming scheme. Former World Jai Alai president John Callahan's body was found in August 1982 inside the trunk of his rented Cadillac in a garage at Miami International Airport in Florida. The forty-five-year-old had two bullet holes in his skull and a dime on his chest. It would be years before Martorano confessed to luring Callahan to Florida and killing him under orders from Bulger (see "The Jai Alai Killings," page 125).

In 1984, the bloodletting took a more grotesque turn when Bulger strangled and shot John McIntyre, a crew member of the Irish gunrunning ship *Valhalla*, whom he suspected of tipping off authorities to the vessel's $1.2 million cargo, a portion of which Bulger had financed to aid the Irish Republican Army. McIntyre's biggest mistake was in telling the wrong police officer that he wanted to talk about Bulger's gunrunning and drug-running operations. That officer told Connolly, who passed the information along to Bulger. Soon, McIntyre was taken to a South Boston home and murdered, his body stripped of teeth to prevent easy identification and buried in the basement. It was the same routine Bulger and Flemmi would use just months later on Deborah Hussey, Flemmi's girlfriend and the daughter of his common-law wife. The twenty-six-year-old Hussey had been threatening to break up with Flemmi and tell her mother about their relationship, which began after he raped her as a teenager. Death put an end to that discussion.

With few repercussions despite a growing list of murders, Bulger and his crew soon turned to something more lucrative—drug dealing. By the 1980s, they were shaking down the state's largest suppliers of marijuana and cocaine. "We never dealt with the street dealers, but rather with a dozen large-scale drug distributors all over the state who were bringing in the coke and marijuana and paying hundreds of thousands to Jimmy," Weeks wrote in his book, *Brutal*.

For years, Whitey Bulger held the dubious distinction of being among the FBI's top wanted men. Authorities circulated various photos of the thug, including one technologically aged photo. *FBI file photo.*

The shakedowns brought thousands of dollars into

**MASSACHUSETTS STATE POLICE**

# MOST WANTE

VIOLENT FUGITIVE
APPREHENSION SEC...

**CATHERINE Elizabeth GREIG**

WANTED FOR:

**HARBORING A FUGITIVE**
(Fugitive - James J. Bulger Jr.)

DOB:..........................4/3/51
Height:........................5'-6"
Weight:.......................130lbs.
Hair:......................Blonde (Dyed)
Eyes:..........................Blue
Complexion:...................Fair
Race:.........................White
Social Security:.........030-40-5309
Peculiarities:...................

AKA's:................Carol Shapeton, Helen
Marshall, Catherine McGonagle

Wanted By the Massachusetts State Police

Catherine Elizabeth Greig was indicted in April 1997 for the harboring of her long time boyfriend, Most Wanted Fugitive James J. Bulger. Bulger a once a notorious "gangster" and a major organized crime figure in the Boston area is wanted for his involvement in (19) nineteen murders. Greig and Bulger have been traveling together since early 1995, shortly after Bulger became a fugitive. Greig is a former dental hygienist who has an affinity for dogs. She is known to exercise regularly and to dye her hair blonde but may have changed her color to avoid capture.

**Massachusetts State Police: Violent Fugitive Apprehension Section**
**1-800-KAPTURE (1-800-527-8873)** or Nights/Weekends (508) 820-2121
www.state.ma.us/msp/wanted/bulger.htm

"HE ESCAPES WHO IS NOT PURSUED" - SOPHOCLES

Authorities had hopes of finding Whitey through his gal pal and companion Catherine Greig. *FBI file photo.*

Bulger's coffers, but it wasn't until July 1991 that he really hit the big time, winning $14 million in the lottery. The Mega Millions ticket, purchased at the South Boston Liquor Mart that he owned, was split between Bulger and two friends and provided each of the winners $89,000 annually for the next twenty years.

By 1994, Bulger's luck was running out. That's when a joint task force composed of the federal Drug Enforcement Administration, the Massachusetts State Police and the Boston Police Department launched a probe into his gaming and drug-dealing operations. The FBI was not advised of the investigation. Within months, authorities had built a federal racketeering case against the South Boston mobster, thanks largely to a number of bookkeepers who agreed to testify against him. On December 23, 1994, Bulger fled Boston with his girlfriend, Theresa Stanley, after Connolly, now retired from the FBI, informed him that sealed indictments had been issued by the Justice Department and his arrest was imminent.

Bulger and Stanley spent about a month traveling together to New York, San Francisco and Los Angeles, using fake identification and tapping into money that Bulger had previously stashed in safety deposit boxes around the country. Stanley soon grew tired of traveling. She missed her children and wanted to go home. Bulger acquiesced, dropping her off at a Boston parking lot. He then met up with another girlfriend, Catherine Greig, who would remain with him for the next sixteen years.

For years, there would be "Whitey" sightings—in London, Toronto and Florida and even coming out of a San Diego theater showing the movie *The Departed*. None panned out. Many Bostonians speculated that the FBI really didn't want to find Bulger, that he would tell tales that would further embarrass the bureau. The FBI did release electronically "aged" photos of Whitey and his gal pal, and in the spring of 2011, the bureau stepped up its campaign with new television and magazine ads, including some directed at plastic surgeons and beauty salons, as Greig was known to be vain about her appearance. On June 22, 2011, ten years after he was placed on the FBI's most wanted list, Bulger and Greig were arrested without incident in Santa Monica, California. An arsenal of weapons, including handguns, an assault rifle and a sawed-off shotgun, and almost $800,000 in cash were found in their two-bedroom, two-bath condo in the Princess Eugenia complex. Bulger returned to Boston within days of his arrest, appearing in U.S. District Court on July 6, 2011, to plead not guilty to forty-eight charges, including nineteen counts of murder, extortion, obstruction of justice, perjury, money laundering, narcotics distribution and weapons charges. Greig faces a single count of harboring a fugitive.

The day few people had ever expected had finally arrived. Whitey Bulger was back in Boston. As he awaits trial in the fall of 2011, his story continues to unfold.

## Chapter 2
# THE MEN IN THE MOB

### THE ANGIULO FAMILY

*Gennaro Angiulo*
*Nickname: "Jerry"*
*Born: March 20, 1919, North End, Boston*
*Died: August 19, 2009, Boston*
*Addresses: 95 Prince Street, Boston; 98 Prince Street, Boston;*
*and Nahant, Massachusetts*
*Association: Patriarca family*

He stood just five feet, seven inches, but a booming voice, wisecracking style and sly yet ruthless temperament gave Gennaro Angiulo an edge among his gangland peers. In the end, however, it would be his fearlessness that finally did him in. One of seven children born to Italian immigrants Caesar and Giovannina Angiulo, Gennaro Angiulo began his life in a brick, walk-up apartment at 95 Prince Street in Boston's North End. He later worked as a clerk in his father's grocery store on Hanover Street, just down the block. By the time he graduated from Boston English High School in 1938, he was talking about becoming a criminal lawyer.

But then the Japanese bombed Pearl Harbor. The attack would change his life.

Enlisting in the U.S. Navy at the start of the war, the young Angiulo would soon see action in the Pacific. Four years later, after achieving the rank of

Gennaro Angiulo was as ruthless as they come. Known for his quick temper and brutality, he rose quickly through the ranks of the New England mob, eventually becoming underboss to Raymond Patriarca, head of the New England crime family. *Courtesy of the Boston Public Library, Print Department.*

chief boatswain's mate, he returned to the North End, where, at the age of twenty-eight, he took a job driving a truck by day and taking bets on horses by night for Massachusetts crime boss Joseph Lombardo (see "Joseph Lombardo," page 50). Always ambitious, Angiulo soon graduated to become a runner for Boston bookies.

# The Men in the Mob

By the early 1950s, trouble was brewing with the numbers racket in Boston. A federal investigation into organized crime, led by Tennessee senator C. Estes Kefauver, had instilled fear in the mob's local leadership. Concerned that the much-publicized panel was on the verge of exposing his dealings, Lombardo ordered all bookmaking operations in Boston to shut down.

In that decision, Angiulo saw an opportunity. Always a sharp businessman when it came to loansharking and gambling, Angiulo approached Lombardo with an offer to take over the mob's betting operations. The boss liked the younger man's chutzpah as much as his ability to churn a profit from the rackets, so he agreed to the offer, cautioning his protégé that he would get no protection should things go wrong. The crime family boss, of course, also got a piece of the action. Within a few years of that agreement, Angiulo's personal wealth hovered around $10 million, authorities estimated.

Flush with cash from his lucrative bookmaking operation, Angiulo soon began eyeing other ventures as a way to launder the proceeds that were steadily flowing into the family till. In 1961, he opened Jay's Lounge in Boston's seedy Combat Zone amid the neon lights of strip joints, gay clubs and tough biker bars. Then, in November 1962, about a year after Angiulo opened the 253 Tremont Street lounge, FBI director J. Edgar Hoover ordered it bugged. In Providence, Rhode Island, the office of New England mob boss Raymond L. S. Patriarca Sr. was bugged too.

By 1963, Angiulo was being publicly identified in congressional hearings as Patriarca's underboss, the second in command of New England. Although he never "made his bones" by killing anyone, Angiulo's friendship with Patriarca had put him among the ranks as a "made man."

The FBI wiretaps in Angiulo's basement office on Tremont Street and at Patriarca's Providence meeting place produced a bounty of information on murders and malfeasance between 1962 and 1965. Among the conversations: an allegation that $5,000 was paid to Massachusetts attorney general Edward W. Brooke to obtain the acquittal of a Patriarca associate, records from that congressional investigation show. Brooke later went on to become the U.S. senator from Massachusetts.

While the wiretaps offered a chilling glimpse into New England's underworld, it was a mob colleague who gave up the organization's intricate secrets—and did the most damage—when he crossed the line to become a federal informant. Joseph "The Animal" Barboza was expecting his hoodlum pals to pick up the $100,000 bail needed to free him from jail on a weapons charge. When they didn't—and when friends started showing up dead—Barboza started talking. By the time he was finished, seven gangsters, including Angiulo and Patriarca, were facing murder, conspiracy or other charges (see "Joseph Barboza," page 34).

At his 1967 arraignment, Angiulo, his eyes framed by dark-rimmed glasses, pleaded not guilty to murder, but it was clear he wasn't hoping for the best. He came to the courthouse carrying a black leather bag containing a toothbrush, toothpaste and shaving gear, newspaper accounts said. He would indeed need those items, given that the judge ordered him held without bail until his trial five months later.

But Angiulo was fortunate. At his January 1968 murder trial, he was acquitted of all charges, despite Barboza's testimony. Two months later, Patriarca wouldn't be as fortunate. He was convicted of murder conspiracy. By the end of a third trial, four mobsters were on death row, two were serving life terms and Patriarca was in the federal penitentiary in Atlanta. With his mentor out of the picture, Angiulo now looked to Ilario "Larry" Zannino, a mob capo, for allegiance. That loyalty would last for decades, and so would Angiulo's good fortune.

In 1969, a grand jury handed up an indictment charging the North End underboss with being an accessory after the fact in connection with a $68,000 armored car heist. The case, however, was tossed out of court following the testimony of a somewhat shaky informant.

Angiulo continued to skirt the law until 1972, when on a star-spangled Fourth of July day, two U.S. Coast Guard members spotted him in Boston Harbor and tried to stop his forty-five-foot yacht for inspection. A three-mile chase ensued, ending in a Dorchester marina where the now seething mobster agreed to let a Coast Guard crew board his vessel.

The inspection yielded three minor violations—failure to stop, failure to carry the boat's registration and harassment of a boarding officer—but Angiulo was having none of it. He crumpled the paperwork and then shoved the twenty-nine-year-old coast guard officer, who promptly arrested the gangster for assault on a federal officer.

After spending the night in jail, Angiulo was hauled into court, where he faced not only a judge but also a courtroom filled with agents from the FBI, IRS and Justice and Treasury Departments. All had come to see the mob underboss. At his trial in May 1973, he was sentenced to just thirty days in jail. It would be the most time Angiulo would spend behind bars in the next ten years.

Still, for both the feds and the mob, the cat and mouse game continued unabated. In 1981, federal investigators caught a break. A judge approved an electronic wiretap that the feds had requested for the gangster's 98 Prince

Street office. It would be Angiulo's colleagues in crime, James "Whitey" Bulger and Stephen "The Rifleman" Flemmi, who would draw the map that investigators used to get into the building. The two snitches, seeing a chance to seize control of Boston's underworld, had been cooperating with

Donato Angiulo had an office on the first floor and lived on the fifth floor of this building at 95 Prince Street in the North End. *Courtesy of the Boston Public Library, Print Department.*

authorities. The court's approval was a coup for the FBI, which had often been confounded in its attempts to use electronic surveillance techniques against the North End hoodlums.

Two years and hundreds of hours of audiotape later, federal agents swooped into Francesco's Restaurant on North Washington Street, where Angiulo was enjoying a late-night dinner with his brothers, Frank and Mike, both of whom had just ordered plates of linguine with clam sauce. As federal agents slapped handcuffs on the three men, Angiulo grew indignant.

"I'll be back before my pork chops get cold," he muttered as he walked out of the restaurant accompanied by federal agents, the local papers trumpeted the next morning. He didn't return.

A third brother, Donato, was arrested just two blocks away from the restaurant as he walked to his car. All four would later be convicted on a slew of charges based on the audio conversations.

Among those taped conversations is one in which Angiulo is heard ordering a hit on a Combat Zone bartender he believed would rat out the organization before a federal grand jury that was investigating the mob's loan-sharking and gambling operations. "I hope it happens tonight," Angiulo is heard saying. "Just hit him in the [expletive] head and stab him, OK? The jeopardy is just a little too much for me. You understand American?" he tells a colleague on the FBI tape.

Whether barking at underlings or ordering a mob hit, Angiulo's own words—and his fearless belief that the feds would never be able to pierce the code of silence that shielded him—helped prosecutors win a conviction. In early 1986, he was sentenced to forty-five years on twelve counts of racketeering, loan-sharking, gambling and obstruction of justice charges.

Yet he never gave up his fight to get out of prison. A capable jailhouse lawyer, he filed several failed appeals, including one in which he argued that he had been framed by the FBI and the agency's two key informants, Bulger and Flemmi.

In July 2007, the U.S. Parole Commission quietly released the frail and sickly eighty-eight-year-old mob kingpin from a federal prison hospital in Devens, Massachusetts, where he was being treated for the kidney disease that would claim his life just two years later.

At his wake and funeral, hundreds lined up along busy Commercial Street for hours just to catch a glimpse of the legendary—and now departed—mob boss. Among the crowd was a veritable who's who of the Boston underworld. As crowds stopped to watch his funeral cortege of Cadillacs, Mercedes and a Rolls Royce carrying Angiulo's widow and children drive slowly along busy

Hanover Street, there was almost a heartfelt sense of finality. Boston's most feared and legendary mobster was dead.

Yet in an ironic twist, at least one of the men who put him behind bars had reason to celebrate. For the day of Angiulo's burial was also Whitey Bulger's eightieth birthday.

*Donato Angiulo*
*Nicknames: "Danny," "Smiley"*
*Born: March 21, 1923, Boston*
*Died: May 3, 2009, Boston*

*Francesco Angiulo*
*Nicknames: "Franky," "Frankie the Cat"*
*Born: 1919*
*Died: August 29, 2009*

*James W. Angiulo*
*Nickname: "Jimmy Jones"*
*Born: 1939*

*Michele Angiulo*
*Nickname: "Mikey"*
*Born: 1927*
*Died: November 29, 2006*

*Vittore Nicolo Angiulo*
*Nicknames: "Nick," "Nicky"*
*Born: 1916*
*Died: September 13, 1987*

They would grow up to become Boston's leading crime family, but out of six Angiulo boys and one girl from the North End neighborhood, only one, Gennaro, would rule as underboss of the Patriarca crime family, controlling the rackets from the 1960s through the mid-1980s in a city once dominated by the Irish mob.

Members of the Patriarca crime family, the brothers grew up in Depression-era Boston amid a tangle of red brick tenements in a North End neighborhood brimming with newly arrived Italian immigrants. A three-story walk-up at 95 Prince Street, located at the corner of Prince and

The Angiulo brothers confer with lawyers in 1964. *Courtesy of the Boston Public Library, Print Department.*

Thatcher Streets, was their home. Their Italian immigrant parents, Caesar and Giovannina Angiulo, owned a grocery store on busy Hanover Street, where their sons worked before finding their own fortunes in real estate, nightclubs and the rackets.

By the 1960s, they were publicly named as members of La Cosa Nostra, running loan-sharking and gambling operations out of 98 Prince Street, just steps away from their childhood home. It was at that Prince Street headquarters where microphones planted by the FBI with the help of Winter Hill mob boss James "Whitey" Bulger and his henchman, Stephen "The Rifleman" Flemmi, captured the brothers as they talked about everything from gambling and loan-sharking operations to murder. In 1986, those taped conversations were used to convict Donato, Gennaro and Francesco Angiulo, the mob's accountant, of racketeering charges. A fourth brother, Michele, was convicted of the lesser charge of illegal gambling.

Despite being nicknamed "Smiley," Donato Angiulo was considered the toughest of the brothers. Known as a ruthless mob lieutenant and money collector, he controlled a crew of Mafia soldiers, often meeting with them at Café Pompeii on Hanover Street to discuss the alignment of gambling territories. Following his 1986 federal trial, he was sentenced to twenty years in prison on racketeering, gambling and loan-sharking charges but was freed in 1997, after eleven years.

Nicolo "Nicky" Angiulo, the oldest of five brothers from Boston's predominantly Italian North End, served as consigliere, or counselor, to the Italian mob in New England. Known as the "family fixer," he kept a low profile until 1983, when he was indicted along with his brothers Gennaro, Donato and Frank on racketeering charges. *Courtesy of the Boston Public Library, Print Department.*

Nicolo Angiulo, the first-born of the brothers, kept a low profile even though he was named family consigliere in 1974. Considered to be the family "fixer," he reportedly had a close relationship with New England mob boss Raymond Patriarca and was said to carry messages between Patriarca and his underboss brother, Gennaro.

Younger brother Francisco, a mob soldier who was in charge of the day-to-day operation of the family's illegal gambling business, was held on $1 million bail upon his racketeering arrest but was free within a month after getting two Indiana insurance companies to post $500,000 bond.

Michele A. Angiulo, a mob associate who served as a trustee in the St. Anthony de Padua Society and an usher at St. Mary's Chapel in the North End, was a loyal churchgoer despite his mob affiliation, friends said. Convicted in 1986 for conducting an illegal gambling business on Prince Street, he was sentenced to three years in prison and fined $5,000 but was released from jail just weeks later by U.S. District Court judge David Nelson after the court received more than two hundred letters praising his character. Among the letters was one from a ten-year-old girl who wrote: "He means an awful lot to me…He's a very nice man." Michele Angiulo's release was overturned that same year by the U.S. Court of Appeals, which found that Judge Nelson had applied "an erroneous standard." Michele was returned to jail to serve out the rest of his sentence.

## JOSEPH BARBOZA

*Alias: Joseph Donati, Joseph Bentley*
*Born: September 20, 1932, New Bedford, Massachusetts*
*Died: February 11, 1976, San Francisco, California*
*Addresses: New Bedford, Massachusetts; Santa Rosa, California*
*Associations: Patriarca family, Winter Hill Gang*

A contract killer considered by authorities to be one of the most powerful and feared figures in Boston's underworld, Joseph "The Animal" Barboza was born to Portuguese immigrants and grew up in the whaling city of New Bedford, Massachusetts, as the second oldest of four children. His father, a middleweight boxer with an eye for the ladies, would later abandon the family, leaving his long-suffering seamstress wife to care for their brood. A street-smart kid, the young Barboza followed in his father's footsteps, briefly pursuing a career as a professional boxer. Later, he worked as a longshoreman and a clerk at a local fruit stand. Swarthy and good-looking, he was adored by women not only for his love of children and animals but also for his "bad boy" image. While he lacked a formal education, he spoke three languages and was a skilled chef who could whip up a native Portuguese dish or a wine-infused French meal at the drop of a hat.

Crime, however, was his real passion. In and out of reform schools since the age of twelve, Barboza was already doing hard time by the time he turned eighteen, when he was imprisoned in the Massachusetts Correctional Institution at Concord in 1950. Three years into his sentence, he orchestrated a prison break by overpowering four guards in what was the largest escape in that institution's history. With seven inmates, including Barboza, on the prowl, there was mayhem in the streets. Trolling Boston's red-light district at Scollay Square, the convicts cruised the bars, attacking and beating innocent bystanders on the street during their first and only night of freedom. The inmates were finally apprehended at an East Boston train station just twenty-four hours after their escape.

It wasn't that brazen escape that caught the eye of the New England mob, however. It was a legendary encounter with a Patriarca crime family underboss at an East Boston bar in 1958, after Barboza was paroled from

Joseph "The Animal" Barboza in one of his early mug shots. *Courtesy of the Boston Public Library, Print Department.*

prison, that really got him noticed. It also earned him the nickname "The Animal."

According to one account, Barboza was reportedly drinking at a Boston-area bar patronized by organized crime figures when an elderly Italian patron, upset by his obnoxious behavior, berated him for his rudeness. Barboza, never one to take criticism lightly, approached the older man and slapped him hard across the face. Sitting nearby, underboss Henry Tameleo angrily shouted to Barboza: "I don't want you to ever slap that man. I don't want you to touch anybody with your hands again." Suddenly, Barboza leaned over and bit the man's ear. "I didn't touch him with my hands," snarled the man who would forevermore be known as "The Animal."

Barboza hooked up with a motley gang of thieves and burglars, supervised by Patriarca soldier Stephen Flemmi. He soon became known for his fearlessness. Within a few years, he had earned his stripes as one of the mob's most prolific contract killers. Because of his Portuguese heritage, however, he was never to become a made man.

By 1966, with a number of hits already under his belt, Barboza had become a reckless liability to his Italian bosses. The final straw came when he sauntered into a nightclub that was paying protection money to underboss Gennaro Angiulo and demanded that he be paid too.

In October 1966, after being arrested on a weapons charge while cruising Boston's Combat Zone with two other hoodlums, Barboza had an epiphany. Held on $100,000 bail, he waited for his mob pals to come up with the money for his release. Nobody did. Then he heard rumors that the Mafia had tipped police off about the guns he was carrying, a misdeed in clear violation of his parole. When two pals, Arthur "Tash" Bratsos and Thomas J. DePrisco, were murdered, Barboza got the message. The two men had collected $59,000 toward his bail when they stopped by the Nite Lite Café in the North End to do a little fundraising. Unfortunately, the duo was shaking down the wrong people. Their bullet-riddled bodies were later found inside the trunk of Bratsos's car dumped in South Boston in an apparent bid to make it look like they were killed by rival Irish gangsters. The money they raised toward Barboza's bail had vanished (see "Arthur Bratsos and Thomas J. DePrisco," page 112).

Realizing an opportunity, the FBI soon began courting Barboza as an informant while he sat brooding in prison, where he was serving a five-year term on the weapons charge. Then, in the summer of 1967, Flemmi made a prison visit that would change the inmate's fate, at least temporarily. Angiulo was making plans to kill him, Barboza's pal and former boss told him. It was a day the FBI had long awaited. The agency had been courting Barboza for months, hoping he would turn informant. In June 1967, he did. Soon Barboza started talking. By the time he was through, seven mobsters, including Patriarca and Angiulo, were indicted on murder and other charges.

In the first of two trials, Angiulo was found not guilty after two hours of jury deliberations. Jurors would later tell reporters they found Barboza's

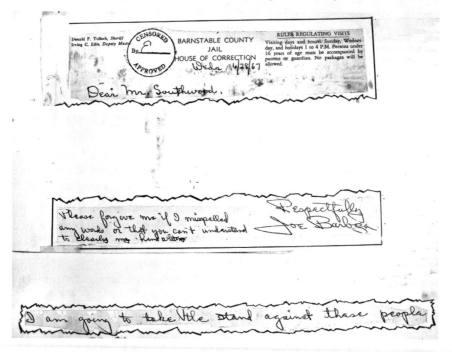

Samples of the letter written by Joseph "The Animal" Barboza indicating that he is willing to rat out the Angiulo and Patriarca families. *Courtesy of the Boston Public Library, Print Department.*

testimony could not be believed. The outcome was far different in the second trial, however, leading to the conviction of Patriarca on conspiracy to murder charges. Shortly after that verdict, Tameleo, who had intervened when Barboza slapped an elderly Italian man in a Revere bar, and Peter Limone, a bodyguard for Angiulo, along with two others, were convicted of the murder of Edward "Teddy" Deegan (see "Edward 'Teddy' Deegan," page 118).

All these convictions didn't sit well with some mob underlings. While the trials were in session, they planted a bomb under the hood of Barboza's black Oldsmobile, which he had given to his attorney, John Fitzgerald, as payment for legal services. Miraculously, Fitzgerald survived the blast but lost his right leg below the knee. The bombing prompted federal officials to begin moving their star witness, now known by the code name "Baron," to secret locations in a bid to protect him, hiding him on a small island off the Massachusetts coast, a military base northwest of Boston and even at Fort Knox, Kentucky, where he stayed in the junior officers' quarters.

The maneuvers worked, albeit only temporarily. Barboza's testimony sent Patriarca to a federal penitentiary in Atlanta, put four mob associates on death row and handed life sentences to two others. In return for his testimony, Barboza was given a one-year prison sentence. In 1969, he was paroled into the new federal Witness Protection Program, becoming the first informant to gain federal protection status. Told to leave Massachusetts forever, Barboza headed to Santa Rosa, California, where he enrolled in culinary school.

Yet killing—like cooking—remained part of his repertoire. Just two years later, in 1971, he pleaded guilty in California to the second-degree murder of a twenty-seven-year-old truck driver in a dispute over stolen bonds. He was sentenced to five years in Folsom Prison, where he became known as an amateur artist and poet, penning verses such as "The Mafia Double Crosses" and "Boston Gang War." His Mafia colleagues, however, never gave up the quest to hunt him down

On February 11, 1976, less than three months after he was released from Folsom Prison, the contract killer who claimed to have murdered twenty-eight men was gunned down by Boston mob capo Joseph "J.R." Russo as Barboza walked to his car in San Francisco. The killer whose raspy voice brought down the head of the New England mob had finally been silenced.

# FILIPPO BUCCOLA (BRUCCOLA)

*Nickname: "Phil"*
*Born: August 6, 1886, Palermo, Sicily*
*Died: 1987, Palermo, Sicily*
*Association: Boston's Sicilian underworld with ties to the Sicilian Mafia*

Phillip or Filippo Buccola (also spelled Bruccola) came to the United States at the age of thirty-two from Palermo, Sicily, where he was born on August 6, 1886. Arriving in the fall of 1920, like many Italian and Sicilian immigrants before him, he moved to Boston, where he became a fight promoter. He is later believed to have headed up a gang of Sicilians in East Boston and was likely a mob player while he was in Sicily.

Educated, affluent and with close ties to La Cosa Nostra in his hometown of Palermo, he quickly rose through the ranks of the underworld in Prohibition-era Boston, eventually assuming the role of head of the Boston faction upon the death of Gaspare Messina.

By 1931, he and his underboss, Joseph Lombardo, were ordering hits, most notably the December 1931 murder of Frank Wallace, the head of the Gustin Gang, who had been hijacking booze-filled trucks and cutting into the Italians' bootlegging profits (see pages 81 and 133). Authorities also suspected he was responsible for the 1933 murder of Jewish mobster Charles "King" Solomon, a prominent bootlegging czar who ran much of the booze-running operations in Boston during the 1920s and early 1930s (see page 76).

In 1932, Frank Morelli, who headed a powerful gang that controlled bootlegging and gambling in Providence, Rhode Island, Maine and Connecticut, merged with Buccola's group to create the New England mob faction. (Morelli's gang is also suspected of being responsible for the 1920 payroll robbery and murders in South Braintree, Massachusetts, that were pinned on Italian anarchists Nicola Sacco and Bartolomeo Vanzetti.) Buccola remained in command of the merged organization until 1954, when he turned over leadership to Raymond L.S. Patriarca Sr. after becoming a target of federal investigators. He moved back to Sicily in 1954, working as a chicken farmer until he died of natural causes at the age of 101 in 1987. Authorities believe he continued to have a hand in Boston's mob affairs, acting as a senior advisor throughout most of his life.

## ELMER FRANCIS BURKE

*Nickname: "Trigger"*
*Born: circa 1918, New York City*
*Died: January 9, 1958, Ossining, New York*
*Affiliations: freelance hit man for hire*

The cold-blooded hit man named Elmer "Trigger" Burke can not be considered a Boston mobster, but when he was brought here for special assignment in 1954, he made his short stay particularly memorable.

Born in Hell's Kitchen, New York, Burke was raised by his brother Charlie after the death of their parents. Burke was soon running afoul of the law, and after service in the U.S. military, he became a hit man for hire. Known as a crazy—even psychotic—killer with a razor-thin temper, Burke coolly shot his best friend, longshoreman Edward "Poochy" Walsh, in a New York bar because of a 1952 beef. He was a suspect in a number of murders and thus considered a reliable gun for hire.

The Charles Street jail was a home away from home for many of the mobsters featured in this book. New York hit man Elmer "Trigger" Burke made a sensational escape in 1954.
*Courtesy of the Boston Public Library, Print Department.*

One of the robbers in the 1950 Brink's heist, Joseph James "Specky" O'Keefe, claimed he'd been cut out of his fair share of the loot and was threatening other gang members. Burke was brought in—possibly by Brink's mastermind Tony Pino—to make sure O'Keefe didn't spill the beans (see "The Brink's Heist," page 113). On June 16, 1954, about 3:00 a.m., O'Keefe was headed to the home of a lady friend, and while walking on Adams Street near Victory Road in Dorchester, he saw a car pull out and follow him. Suddenly, machine gun fire exploded around him. O'Keefe ran for his life through the neighborhood, returning fire as he ducked for cover. A bullet hit his watch, tearing it from his wrist, but miraculously, he sustained only minor wounds, although police later followed a trail of blood through the neighborhood. Awakened residents thought a gang war had broken out. A shaken O'Keefe went into hiding. Bizarrely, Burke did not leave Boston. A day later, a Boston police patrolman, alerted by New York police that Burke was in the area, saw the suspected triggerman in the Back Bay and managed to arrest him without incident. A veritable arsenal was found in Burke's room in a Back Bay boardinghouse.

With a strange pride and exhibiting wacky behavior that could have been an act, Burke bragged about shooting O'Keefe and babbled about himself in the third person, particularly about a child he had seen on the street that night. "If Burke had killed that kid, Burke would have killed himself. I'm glad Burke didn't kill that kid." Burke was probably dismayed to learn that he had failed to kill Specky. The attempts on O'Keefe's life finally convinced Specky to rat out his fellow Brink's robbers.

Burke cooled his heels in the Suffolk County Jail on Charles Street in Boston, but not for long. In August, in a flawless operation, the man described as a "kill-crazy psychopath" escaped, aided by three men who managed to get through four locked doors to reach the jail's exercise area, where they rushed him to an escape car. Burke had walked through the jail "like a ghost," as the *Boston Globe* reported. The spectacular escape rocked Boston.

Burke only had another year of freedom. On August 28, 1955, he was arrested in South Carolina and returned to New York. He was tried for the murder of Poochy Walsh, convicted and sentenced to death. On January 9, 1958, he was electrocuted at Sing Sing prison.

Two Boston men, Allen G. Locke of Back Bay and William E. Cavanaugh of Jamaica Plain, were convicted and sentenced to seven to ten years in state prison for helping Burke escape. Today, the Charles Street jail where the hoodlum was once incarcerated has been transformed into the swanky Liberty Hotel.

## JOHN CONNOLLY

*Nickname: Zip*
*Born: August 1, 1940, Boston*
*Addresses: 165 Quincy Shore Drive, Quincy; Ridgewood Drive, Milton*
*Affiliation: FBI*

He once was known for his expensive suits and polished appearance. He was a law enforcement star, crediting with taking down Boston's Italian mob with his insider knowledge of Boston Irish gangs. In the end, FBI agent John Connolly's romance with the dark side caught up with him and tarnished not only his reputation but that of the entire bureau.

Connolly grew up in South Boston, near the same projects as had James "Whitey" Bulger. He joined the FBI in 1968. In the mid-1970s, according to later court records, Connolly approached Whitey about being an informant, and the relationship deepened to include gifts, dinners and exchanges of information. It grew more tortured and complicated as Connolly authorized

The Harbor Point Housing Project, childhood home of John Connolly, now the site of a luxury waterfront community, still looks much the same as it did when Connolly was growing up in "the projects." *Photo by Beverly Ford.*

payments to his informants and other FBI agents—including Connolly's boss, John Morris—were pulled into the circle of corruption.

Connolly reportedly tipped off Bulger and his cohorts about their enemies and shielded him from prosecution; state and local police had long wondered why their investigations against Whitey went nowhere. A prime example of Connolly's efforts is that of the case of Brian Halloran, a hood approached by Whitey and Stephen Flemmi to kill World Jai Alai businessman Roger Wheeler, who suspected the Irish mob of cutting into profits at his Connecticut Jai Alai operation (see "The Jai Alai Killings," page 125). Halloran's offer to talk to the FBI went nowhere, and he ended up slain.

But Connolly's chief favor to Whitey came after he had retired from the FBI. In 1994, Connolly told Bulger that he was about to be indicted. Bulger went into hiding and remained at large for the next sixteen years while Connolly's life unraveled. Hints that Connolly's relationships with his informants went too far had surfaced over the years in Boston newspapers, but the FBI had brushed them off.

Looking back, it's hard to believe that Connolly, who retired from the FBI in 1990, thought he could just retire and fade away into the sunset, but then again, so many others had done just that in Boston. In the late 1990s, when other gangsters started talking to investigators, Connolly's efforts on behalf of his mobster friends were suddenly subjected to the harsh light of day. In 2002, Connolly was convicted of racketeering and obstruction of justice and, in 2008, of second-degree murder. Former FBI supervisor John Morris testified in exchange for immunity. Connolly is now serving a life sentence.


# VINCENT FERRARA

*Nicknames: "The Animal," "Vinny Nip"*
*Born: 1949, Boston's North End*
*Address: Revere, Massachusetts*
*Association: Patriarca family*


An up-and-comer in the local Mafia, Vincent Ferrara was a capo to his mob pals and "a very dangerous man" to pursuing investigators, who nicknamed him "The Animal" because of his fierceness.

Not much is known about Ferrara's early life, but by 1985, he was already becoming a standout in Mafia circles for allegedly ordering a hit on his longtime friend Vincent "Jimmy" Limoli, another mob capo, as part of a bloody power struggle for dominance within the New England mob. Ferrara was sentenced to twenty-two years for that slaying but was freed after sixteen years in prison when U.S. District Court judge Mark L. Wolf found that the U.S. Attorney's Office had withheld evidence provided by a key witness who later tried to recant claims that the mob captain directed his co-defendant to murder Limoli. In making that decision, Wolf said Ferrara was denied due process and may not have agreed to a plea deal had he known about the recantation. Assistant U.S. attorney Jeffrey Auerhahn, who prosecuted Ferrara based on the tainted evidence, remains on the job as a federal prosecutor and has never been publicly reprimanded or disciplined. Wolf, however, referred Auerhahn to the Massachusetts Bar Council, which in 2010 agreed to review the voluminous records filed in the case before deciding whether to impose sanctions against the twenty-five-year Justice Department veteran.

It's not that Ferrara wasn't ruthless. In 1987, just two years after that murder, he ordered Boston bookie Harry "Doc Jasper" Sagansky to report to Vanessa's, a sandwich shop in the Prudential Center in Boston's Back Bay that had been secretly bugged by the FBI. Once there, Ferrara demanded $500,000 as tribute from the elderly bookie. "Kid, I'm eighty-nine years old. How long am I gonna be in business?" Sagansky responded, according to *Boston Herald* columnist Howie Carr. Ferrara shrugged and told Sagansky he would hold the bookie's aide, Moe Weinstein, as collateral. Sagansky delivered $250,000 in cash to Ferrara the next day inside the lobby of a Boston hotel, and Weinstein was released, Carr notes.

By 1989, it was clear he had made his way to the top of Mafia circles. That's when he became a made man in a secret Mafia induction ceremony held at a Medford home and clandestinely recorded by the FBI. It was Ferrara's closing words that lent a bit of irony to the solemn occasion. "Only the ghost knows what really took place over here today by God," he said as the ceremony ended, according to a transcript of that Mafia induction.

Make that God and the FBI.


## STEPHEN FLEMMI

*Nickname: "The Rifleman"*
*Addresses: 25 Ambrose Street, Roxbury, Massachusetts; 832 East Third Street, South Boston, Massachusetts; and 799 East Third Street, South Boston, Massachusetts*
*Born: June 9, 1934, Boston*
*Association: Winter Hill Gang, Patriarca family*

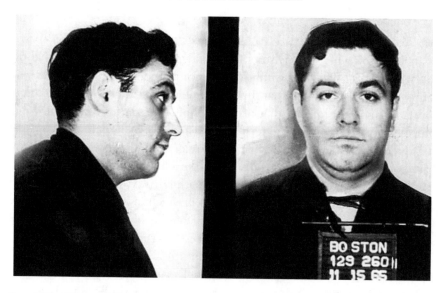

Steve "The Rifleman" Flemmi in 1969. *Courtesy of the Boston Public Library, Print Department.*

His marksmanship as an army sharpshooter earned Stephen Flemmi the nickname "The Rifleman," but when it came to mob hits, his aim was dead-on too. Although not the most prolific mob hit man, the five-foot, eight-inch, 140-pound Flemmi had a reputation as a tough killer who would mow down anyone—even a trio of brothers—if asked.

The eldest of two brothers, he was born in Roxbury, Massachusetts, the son of Italian immigrants Giovanni, a bricklayer, and his homemaker wife, Mary Irene. Like many immigrants, Flemmi's father, a proud veteran of the Royal Italian Army during World War I, found a home for the family in Orchard Park, a series of three-story brick tenements on the fringe of South Boston.

It was there, on the streets of Roxbury, where Flemmi met his lifelong friend Frank Salemme, better known as "Cadillac Frank" because of his taste in cars. The two would later go into the loan-sharking business together and eventually become a hit man tag team for both the Italian and Irish mobs. By the time Stephen was seventeen, however, he was looking for a way out of the poverty plaguing the Boston neighborhood he called home. His escape came in the form of the Korean War.

As an army enlistee at the age of seventeen, he saw his share of battles. In fact, during two tours of duty with the 187th Infantry Regiment and a stint as a paratrooper, Flemmi showed such fearlessness that he was awarded both the Silver and Bronze Stars for bravery. He later joined the International

Association of Airborne Veterans, which organized tours that allowed him to parachute with foreign airborne forces at locations throughout the world.

When Flemmi returned from Korea, he and his younger brother Vincent, known as Jimmy, hooked up with Joseph Barboza, a Portuguese American hoodlum with ties to both the Italian and Irish mobs. It was a tough balancing act for Barboza, but by the time a gang war broke out between the two groups, he had aligned himself with the Irish faction, better known as Somerville's Winter Hill Gang.

The gangland war turned into a lucrative business deal for the three unlikely pals, who by now had become contract killers. In 1965, Stephen Flemmi forged another alliance, again with an unlikely partner. FBI agent H. Paul Rico was hoping to glean information about Boston's gangland scene from the contract shooter, but it was Flemmi who got the better deal. In exchange for providing tips to his FBI handler, Flemmi managed to get members of the rival Charlestown mob arrested while providing protection to his friends.

Yet loyalty can be fleeting when it involves gangsters. Barboza found that out in 1967, when the mob left him cooling his heels in jail, where he was being held on $100,000 bail on a weapons charge. Under pressure by FBI agents to turn state's evidence, Barboza resisted cooperating. Then he learned that two buddies who had been raising money to get him released had been rubbed out, their bodies found in the trunk of a car in South Boston (see "Arthur Bratsos and Thomas J. DePrisco," page 112). Convinced that he was next on the hit list, Barboza agreed to cooperate with Agent Rico.

Barboza's decision bothered Flemmi. He was convinced that Barboza's attorney, John Fitzgerald, had persuaded his client to become a witness against the mob. In retaliation, Flemmi and Salemme arranged to have a bomb planted under the hood of Fitzgerald's car, which Barboza had given him as payment toward legal fees. When the attorney turned the key to the car, the explosion that occurred shook the rafters and cracked the windows of homes within blocks of the blast. Miraculously, Fitzgerald survived, but he lost a leg in the 1968 murder attempt.

When it became clear that Flemmi and Salemme were responsible for the bombing, Flemmi's FBI handler, Agent Rico, advised Flemmi to leave town. He did, taking with him his childhood friend Salemme and a two-bit hoodlum named Peter Poulos, a witness to the 1967 murder of one of the Bennett brothers (see "The Bennett Brothers," page 109). Salemme bailed out of the trip in Los Angeles, fleeing to New York City, while Flemmi and Poulos headed to Las Vegas. Only Flemmi arrived. Poulos's bullet-riddled body, with three .38-caliber slugs to the head, was found in 1969 in the desert outside Las Vegas.

"The desert's not soft," Flemmi told Salemme shortly after the Poulos murder, recounting an attempt to bury his victim's body.

"What were you thinking, it's the Sahara? This is Nevada. This isn't North Africa," Salemme replied, recounting that conversation before House Government Reform Committee investigators in 2003.

No one would ever be charged with Poulos's murder. In fact, authorities claim their investigation was thwarted not by the mob but by the FBI, which was protecting Flemmi and his close pal James "Whitey" Bulger.

By 1972, things had quieted down in Boston. Agent Rico, still in touch with Flemmi, called him in Montreal, Canada, where the mobster was hiding out, and urged him to return home. Everything would be forgotten, the FBI agent told his informant. It was. When Flemmi returned to Boston, the charges against him in the car bombing case were dismissed. Salemme, who worked the streets as a bookmaker, loan shark and enforcer with Flemmi, took the rap instead and ended up behind bars.

Still, the hits didn't stop. Sometimes Flemmi would do the killing. Other times, he would play undertaker for Whitey Bulger's murderous rages. By

The house on East Third Street in South Boston where the body of Stephen Flemmi's sometime girlfriend Deborah Hussey was buried. Her body was later dug up from the basement grave and buried near the Neponset River in Quincy after this home was put up for sale. *Photo by Beverly Ford.*

the 1980s, they had killed fifteen more victims. One of them was Flemmi's girlfriend, a stunning blonde he met when she was just seventeen. Flemmi lavished Debra Davis with cars, clothes and jewelry, but by the time she was twenty-six, she had fallen in love with another man and was looking for a way out of the relationship. In 1981, Flemmi lured Davis to a vacant South Boston home he had just purchased for his parents, where Bulger strangled her. Flemmi would later cut off her fingertips and pull out her teeth to prevent her body from being identified.

Four years later, in 1985, Flemmi and Bulger killed another Flemmi girlfriend, Deborah Hussey, who was also his stepdaughter, in the same fashion after luring her to the same East Third Street home, where she was strangled by Bulger. The trio then buried her remains in the basement of a second home on the same street. The attractive twenty-six-year-old brunette had been Flemmi's girlfriend ever since he raped her when she was just a teenager. But in the days before her murder, she had grown tired of the nearly fifty-year-old mobster and was on the verge of breaking up with him and telling her mother, Flemmi's common-law wife, about their relationship.

Bulger's protégé Kevin Weeks, who helped dispose of Hussey's body, later wrote about the murder in his 2006 book *Brutal: The Untold Story of My Life Inside Whitey Bulger's Irish Mob*: "Stevie said he'd take care of the clothes and the teeth. He was all business, going about the task of removing, cleaning up and pulling teeth," Weeks recalled. "Even though he had a long term relationship with Debbie, this wasn't bothering him any more than it had bothered Jimmy. Stevie was actually enjoying it, the way he always enjoyed a good murder."

Around the same time, Bulger and Flemmi were working as FBI informants, feeding investigators information about their Italian rivals, including giving up the floor plans to Gennaro Angiulo's 98 Prince Street office. The floor plans would come in handy when the FBI planted listening devices in the Italian mob boss's headquarters in 1986, leading to the arrest of Angiulo and his brothers in an investigation that would take down Boston's Italian faction (see "Gennaro Angiulo," page 25).

By 1990, mob operations in Boston had been decimated, and the feds were looking at other targets, notably Bulger and Flemmi. In 1995, Flemmi was facing federal charges for racketeering and extortion, allegations that he found absurd, given his claims that the FBI had granted the two mobsters permission to commit certain crimes short of murder while they were working as informants. The court hearings that followed unearthed some of the Boston FBI's deepest, darkest secrets, including allegations that agents had accepted payoffs and leaked information to protect the two informants.

A judge later ruled the pair had received no promise of immunity and, in August 2001, sentenced Flemmi to ten years in prison for money laundering and extortion as part of a plea deal with prosecutors.

In a bid to escape the death penalty, Flemmi pleaded guilty in 2004 to ten murders, including killings in Florida and Oklahoma, in exchange for a life sentence. He also began cooperating with investigators now probing the FBI's handling of informants. Among the information he supplied were allegations that he and Bulger paid former FBI agent John "Zip" Connolly $200,000 in cash and gave cash and other gifts to other FBI agents and police. Sentenced to a life term with no chance for parole, Flemmi is no longer in a federal prison as of late 2011. His whereabouts are unknown.

## VINCENT JAMES FLEMMI

*Nicknames: "Jimmy the Bear," "The Bear," "Big Bear"*
*Born: September 5, 1935, Boston*
*Died: October 16, 1979*
*Associations: Winter Hill Gang, Patriarca family*

Vincent "Jimmy the Bear" Flemmi, brother of Steve "The Rifleman" Flemmi. *Courtesy of the Boston Public Library, Print Department.*

While not as notorious as his brother Stephen "The Rifleman," Vincent James Flemmi could be just as lethal, and he, too, became a FBI informant, even while terrorizing enemies in Boston's underworld. A bank robber and enforcer, he played a key role in Boston's Irish mob wars of the 1960s and 1970s, survived attempts on his life in 1964 and 1965 and achieved, in the words of Suffolk County district attorney Garrett H. Byrne, "a record a mile long." With Joseph "The Animal" Barboza, he took out Edward "Teddy" Deegan in 1964 and was a frequent companion to hit man Johnny Martorano. He once decapitated one of his victims (see "The Irish Mob Wars," page 120). He

A mug shot of Vincent "Jimmy the Bear" Flemmi in his twenties. *Courtesy of the Boston Public Library, Print Department.*

had a volatile temper and was alleged to have beat someone who did not let him cut in line. While known to be an addict, he was tenacious. When he survived a stabbing in prison, a police desk clerk said, "He's got more lives than a cat," according to the *Boston Globe* in 1979. He died at age forty-seven of a drug overdose in a cell on October 16, 1979, serving an eleven-to seventeen-year sentence for armed assault with intent to murder.

## JOSEPH LOMBARDO

*Nickname: "Big Joe L."*
*Alias: "Joseph Lombardi"*
*Address: 317 Hanover Street, North End, Boston; Bettinson Avenue, Everett,*
*Massachusetts*
*Born: circa 1897, Salemi, Sicily*
*Died: July 17, 1969*
*Affiliation: Patriarca family*

Little is known about the history of the New England mob between the 1930s and the 1950s, when Joseph Lombardo rose to power in the tenement-lined streets of Boston's North End. A consigliere to boss Phillip Buccola from 1931 to 1954, Lombardo gained renewed respect when three days before Christmas 1931, he knocked off the Gustin Gang in a dispute over bootlegging, ending the Irish mob's reign. The hit, which brought the Italians into power in Boston, helped shape the New England Mafia, changing the way it was perceived nationally among other organized crime families.

A 1925 photo of Joseph Lombardo of the Lombardo gang graces this police poster issued after the gang killed members of the Gustin Gang in the 1930s.
*Courtesy of the Boston Public Library, Print Department.*

According to *The Underboss* by Dick Lehr and Gerard O'Neill, Lombardo "became an almost mythical figure, a man of respect who could arbitrate the endless childish squabbles among his underlings over money and territory." Known by his initials, J.L., Lombardo had "the bearing and manner of leadership, a

Pasquale Lombardo, brother of Joseph Lombardo, was detained in the Frank Wallace murder but was released after questioning by police. *Courtesy of the Boston Public Library, Print Department.*

street-toughness and Old World geniality that makes those who remember him nostalgic for his era," the authors write.

After killing off Gustin Gang head Frank Wallace and his enforcer at a Hanover Street building where Lombardo's business, C&F Importing, was located, the mobster went underground, disappearing for nine days before surrendering to authorities on New Year's Eve. Questioned by police, the mobster politely refused to answer, apologizing for his lack of cooperation, Lehr and O'Neill write. A Suffolk grand jury later freed him and two others charged in the Gustin slayings.

He returned to the North End to run a restaurant, as well as the mob's gambling and loan-sharking operations, for the next thirty years. He retired from mob business in 1954 and later moved out of Boston to the city of Everett, where he died of natural causes at age seventy-two in 1969.

## VINCENT MICHAEL MARINO

*Nickname: "Gigi"*
*Aliases: Vinnie "Gigi" Portalla*
*Born: circa 1962*
*Address: Nahant, Massachusetts*
*Association: Patriarca family*

Say the name Vincent Michael Marino and it's likely to induce chuckles among mobsters and lawmen alike. Certainly the hits he arranged and the terror he induced are no laughing matter, but what happened while Marino was being arrested made him the butt of jokes for weeks.

At six feet tall and 220 pounds, Marino, better known as "Gigi" Portalla, was an imposing character. The drug user and fierce mob enforcer even talked about taking over the Patriarca crime family by killing Frank Salemme, who once served as acting boss of the New England faction. He was on the short list of suspects in the shooting of Salemme at a Saugus pancake house in 1989. Charges against him in that case were later dropped when a jury failed to convict him. Yet all that talk and suspicion about murdering the mob boss gave Salemme loyalists other ideas. It was time to get the troublesome Marino out of the picture.

What began as a murder attempt in the early morning hours of November 24, 1996, turned into an incident that would be remembered in the annals of mob history not for its brutishness but for its noir humor. The incident began around 1:00 a.m., when Marino and his driver, Charles McConnell, arrived at the Caravan Club in Revere. As they got out of their car, a series of gunshots rang out, shattering windows and frightening the club's 150 patrons. In a desperate bid to get away from the shooters, believed to be Salemme's pals, Marino scrambled to get inside the packed club. Bleeding heavily from a gunshot to the buttocks, he collapsed on the dance floor. Wounded in the arm and back, McConnell drove to the nearby Wonderland Ballroom, where he told police about the Caravan Club shooting. About fifteen minutes later, another Marino driver and enforcer, Robert Nogueira, stepped into the parking lot of a Comfort Inn hotel in Saugus and was shot ten times, dying on the pavement almost immediately.

Less than three weeks later, Drug Enforcement Administration agents arrested Marino and McConnell on cocaine trafficking charges at Logan International Airport in Boston. While talking with Marino, a DEA agent jokingly asked him to sign a consent form authorizing the removal of a tracking device from his buttocks that government doctors had implanted to make him easier to follow during treatment for his wounds. Marino was stunned. At his arraignment on the drug trafficking charge, he told a federal magistrate that the feds had "implanted a microphone" in his rear end during recent surgery. Then he told family members to contact the American Civil Liberties Union.

Soon, the story made the rounds in newspapers and the talk show circuit. The question everyone wanted to know was: Did the feds really wire the mobster's butt? An X-ray would later find some type of foreign object in his abdomen but no proof that he had been microchipped by the feds.

After the judge in the case ordered the government to fess up about whether it had indeed implanted a biochip in Marino's nether regions, U.S. attorney Donald Stern issued a tongue-in-cheek response. "We can confirm the U.S. Drug Enforcement Administration did not implant a tracking device in defendant Vincent M. 'Gigi Portalla' Marino's buttocks. We cannot speak, however, for any extraterrestrial beings. I hope this will finally put the matter *behind* us," Stern said.

It didn't. Marino was convicted and sentenced to thirty-five years in prison on racketeering and drug charges in April 2000. In an ironic twist, Marino was convicted on the same day that former FBI agent John Connolly was indicted on charges of obstruction of justice, racketeering and conspiring with criminals.

## James Martorano

*Born: December 10, 1941, Cambridge, Massachusetts*
*Affiliations: Patriarca family, Winter Hill Gang*

The younger brother of hit man Johnny Martorano, James seemed destined for a different career. Like his brother, he played football and graduated from Milton High School in 1959 (his older brother was kept back, so they were in the same graduation class). James got a diploma from Boston College on an athletic scholarship, but then he, too, was pulled into the shady enterprises that would claim his brother's attention. On November 10, 1964, James Martorano was at Luigi's, his father's bar, when a divorced thirty-five-year-old waitress, Margaret Sylvester, was found beaten and stabbed to death, her body stuffed in a sack in the restaurant's loft. Johnny would eventually murder two people who might have implicated his brother in her death. James had his own schemes, and in 1979, he was convicted of fixing horse races with other Winter Hill Gang members. Released in 1986, he attempted to pursue various business ventures and, according to his brother's memoir, is now a winemaker.

## JOHN VINCENT MARTORANO

*Nickname: "The Executioner"*
*Alias: Richard Aucoin*
*Born: December 13, 1940, Cambridge, Massachusetts*
*Affiliations: Winter Hill Gang, Whitey Bulger's crew*

With twenty known murders on his résumé, John Vincent Martorano was one of Boston's most lethal thugs, a hit man for hire with both charisma and a dead aim. An enforcer for the Winter Hill Gang, he was close to Whitey Bulger and Stephen Flemmi, taking orders from them with few questions. Above all, he professed to hate "rats"—that is, the guys who turn on their friends by giving them up to police. But like so many wise guys, faced with hard time and perceived betrayals, he would eventually open his mouth and reveal to the world the depths of Bulger's and Flemmi's murderous ways—and his own.

Johnny Martorano was born into a middle-class family to an Irish mother and Italian father and grew up in the Boston suburbs with his

brother Jimmy, who was just eleven months younger. He attended grammar school with Bill Delahunt, who would go on to be a state senator and Norfolk County district attorney; they were altar boys together. He was a standout football player (as was his brother), and after graduating from Milton High School in 1959, he helped out at his family's restaurant, Luigi's, in Boston's Combat Zone, the red-light district. By age twenty-five, he had committed his first murder and would soon develop a reputation as a reliable, cunning and fearless hit man for hire. His brother Jimmy also wracked up his own body count.

Johnny Martorano in 1963. *Courtesy of the Boston Public Library, Print Department.*

# The Men in the Mob

Martorano's first hit was in November 1962, when he killed thirty-two-year-old Robert Palladino to silence him from possibly implicating his brother Jimmy for murdering a waitress; Palladino's body was dumped at North Station. Other hits followed: Joseph J. Notarageli, thirty-five, was shot at lunchtime while sitting in a restaurant in Medford Square, just a bit outside of Boston, on April 19, 1973; James "Spike" O'Toole, a rival gang member, was killed in December 1973; Tommy King, who had feuded with Whitey, was taken out in November 1975 (see "Neponset River Bridge," page 105); Richard J. Castucci was killed on December 29, 1976, for ratting out members of the Winter Hill Gang; and John W. Jackson, another potential witness to Jimmy's waitress slaying, was killed in September 1966.

In a particularly heinous case, Martorano was told to take care of Herbert "Smitty" Smith, a manager at the Basin Street South club in Roxbury. Smitty, an African American, had a run-in with Stephen Flemmi, who frequented the mostly black club. In the wee hours of Saturday, January 6, 1968, Martorano came upon the forty-seven-year-old Smitty in his car with two passengers on Normandy and Brunswick Streets in Roxbury. Without hesitation, he shot everyone in the car. The passengers were nineteen-year-old Elizabeth Dickson and seventeen-year-old Douglas Barrett, innocent bystanders in the wrong place at the wrong time. Dickson still clutched a package of cigarettes, and there was a trail of blood on Normandy Street. "Police Seek Motive in Bizarre Slaying of 3," the *Boston Globe* declared. But the victims were all black, and in Boston's racially tinged culture, the murders were soon forgotten—until Martorano confessed to them.

Murder begat murder. On June 12, 1975, Eddie Connors, age forty-two, a former New England Middleweight champion and owner of two taverns, was found gunned down in a phone booth on Morrissey Boulevard in Dorchester, the phone receiver still swinging back and forth. Connors, an ex-con, was awaiting trial on an armed robbery charge. Martorano later said that Whitey and Flemmi carried out the hit, meant to silence Connors from talking about the Spike O'Toole murder, and Martorano drove the getaway car.

In 1978, Martorano had eighteen murders to his tally, and he fled to Florida, where he attempted to live a quiet life. But he was tapped to do two more jobs. On May 27, 1981, he shot and killed businessman Roger Wheeler in Tulsa, Oklahoma, at the behest of Bulger, who feared Wheeler would learn of profit-skimming from the jai alai gambling business. Then, when Bulger feared that James Callahan, the former president of World Jai Alai, was a liability, Martorano took care of him, too. His body was found in the trunk of a car at a Miami airport in August 1982 (see "The

Jai Alai Killings," page 125). Martorano would later say that he felt "lousy" about the hit and that he didn't want to kill a guy whom he had killed someone for earlier.

Martorano was arrested and tried in 1998 with Frank Salemme, Stephen Flemmi and others on a variety of charges. He pleaded guilty to twenty murders spanning three states and three decades and testified against Bulger, Connolly and others. In a controversial deal, he got twelve years in prison—seemingly a slap on the wrist for his twenty murders—because prosecutors were more anxious to nail Bulger and Flemmi.

In 2007, Martorano was released from prison. Declining witness protection, he returned to Boston, where, he claimed, he wanted to make a new start with his family. He appeared on CBS's *60 Minutes* (it was, he said, a favor to the late Ed Bradley, an acquaintance when both played high school football). Correspondent Steve Kroft asked him for his hit count. "I confessed to twenty in court," Martorano said. "You sure you remembered them all?" Kroft asked. "I hope so," was the reply. Later, Martorano sat down with *Boston Herald* columnist Howie Carr for interviews that formed the basis for Carr's 2011 book, *Hitman: The Untold Story of Johnny Martorano*. Carr writes that the interviews were held on Sunday mornings in the *Herald* newsroom, where one of Carr's colleagues commented on how "damned likable" the murderous thug seemed to be.

Some of the families of his victims, however, may find it hard to comprehend that Martorano was a free man—and living in Boston, no less—after his trail of blood.

## JAMES J. McLEAN

*Nickname: "Buddy"*
*Born: 1930 (or 1929)*
*Died: October 31, 1965*
*Address: Snow Terrace, Somerville*
*Affiliation: Winter Hill Gang*

"He looks like a choir boy but fights like the devil." This is how an unnamed associate described James "Buddy" McLean to author T.J. English for his book on Irish mobs, *Paddy Whacked*.

McLean was an orphan who was reared by immigrant Portuguese parents. He worked as a longshoreman in Charlestown and East Boston, where he

# The Men in the Mob

The bucolic setting of City Square Park in Charlestown belies the neighborhood's notorious past. Just steps from here, racketeer Bernard "Bernie" McLaughlin was gunned down on October 31, 1961, while walking on Chelsea Street during broad daylight by Winter Hill boss James "Buddy" McLean. *Photo by Stephanie Schorow.*

developed a reputation for being a tough fighter but a fair man. Moving to the Winter Hill area of Somerville, he oversaw a crew of hoodlums who ran a host of enterprises from gambling to loan-sharking. He had attempted to settle matters with Charlestown thugs after George McLaughlin was brutally beaten up following an altercation on Salisbury Beach on Labor Day 1961 (see "The Irish Mob Wars," page 120). The McLaughlins were set on vengeance, but McLean wouldn't allow it. McLean later found his car wired to explode. He took preemptive action. On October 31, 1961, he shot Bernie McLaughlin near City Square in Charlestown. The gang war was now engaged in earnest. Other deaths soon followed, as newspapers kept a running tally and speculated about the identities of the killers and the reasons for the slayings, which seemed to make little sense. The McLaughlin brothers were finished off by 1965. Ten days after the death of the last McLaughlin, McLean was leaving a Somerville bar on Broadway near Marshall Street in the wee hours with three companions when, according to patrolman Edward Kiley, quoted in the *Boston Globe*, McLean walked up to the policeman and rubbed his badge, saying, "That's for luck." A few moments later, as another policeman watched, a man stepped out of the shadows and fired at McLean and his companions. McLean tried to draw his .38 but was cut down before he could get off a shot. The policemen gave chase but lost the gunman when he ran through an alleyway to a getaway car waiting on Sewall Street. The Hughes brothers of Charlestown, allies of the McLaughlins, apparently did the hit. With McLean gone, Howie Winter would take over the gang. Both Hughes brothers would be slain within two years.

## ANGELO MERCURIO

*Nickname: Sonny*
*Born: 1936*
*Died: December 11, 2006*
*Affiliation: Patriarca family, Winter Hill Gang*

Angelo "Sonny" Mercurio, a native of Boston's West End, was a small-time player in Boston's gangland landscape but achieved fame for one act of betrayal. In 1989, he informed the FBI of an upcoming Mafia induction ceremony arranged by Raymond "Junior" Patriarca in Medford. The feds convinced him to wear a wire, and the entire ceremony was taped for posterity. It was a coup for Mercurio's handler, FBI agent John Connolly. Mercurio even turned down the sound of the television so the reception for the bug would be better. Mercurio, who had a number of run-ins with the law, allegedly became an FBI informant in the 1980s. He died in 2006 under the federal Witness Protection Program. Published reports indicate that he may have regretted the role he played in taking down the Patriarca organization.

## GASPARE MESSINA

*Born: 1879, Salemi, Sicily*
*Died: 1957, Somerville, Massachusetts*
*Addresses: 330 North Street, Boston, Massachusetts;*
*275 North Street, Boston, Massachusetts*
*Association: early Boston mob*

Gaspare Messina arrived at Ellis Island in 1905 with waves of other Italian immigrants, all looking to trade the poverty of their homeland for a nation rich with the promise of prosperity. With his wife, Francesca, his brother

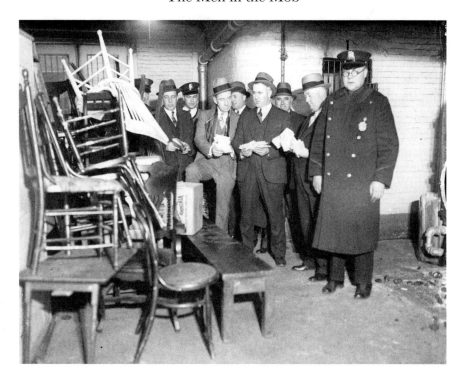

Police inventory articles seized during the raid on a bookie's operation at 1 Boylston Street in this Leslie Jones photo taken on March 23, 1932. *Courtesy of the Boston Public Library, Print Department.*

Phillip and Phillip's wife, Giovanna, whom his brother would soon abandon, he settled in Brooklyn, likely in one of the tenement neighborhoods populated by other Sicilians that had sprung up with the immigrant influx.

Father to a daughter, Gasparina, and three sons, Salvatore, Luciano and Vito, Messina and his wife, along with Giovanna, moved in about 1918 to Boston, where, among storefronts filled with Italian delicacies and sidewalks leading into a labyrinth of brick tenements, he ruled during the early years of Prohibition as head of the Boston Mafia until 1924. It was during those years that Messina hooked up with Frank Cucchiara, who was later to become a consigliere to the Patriarca crime family, and Paolo Pagnotta to form G. Messina & Co., a wholesale grocery business on Prince Street in Boston's North End. By the late 1920s, he had added another title to his name: president of the Neptune Oil Corporation. Although he assumed a businessman's role, Messina remained true to his mob roots. While he gave up his role as Boston's don in 1924, by the time the decade ended, he was back in the game.

By the early 1930s, he had been named capo di capi, "boss of all bosses," by the mob membership who were trying to resolve a dispute among the Mafia's New York, Buffalo and Midwest families. The disagreement turned into what was to become known as the Castellammarese War. Eager to end the bloodshed, Messina called a grand council meeting in Boston, but his efforts were futile. The bloody power struggle over control of the Mafia continued until about 1932. Eventually, fellow Sicilian and former fight promoter Filippo "Phil" Buccola was named head of the Boston family. Buccola ruled until 1954.

Messina, who rose from the huddled Sicilian masses to start the Boston mob faction, died in 1957, his great American dream of success fulfilled.

## PATRICK NEE

*Born: 1943, Ros Muc, County Galway, Ireland*
*Address: South Boston*
*Affiliation: Mullen Gang*

Just a few years after his family immigrated to South Boston from Ireland, fourteen-year-old Patrick Nee hooked up with the Mullen Gang and later led the group in its battles with another Southie gang, the Killeens. He served as a U.S. Marine, including a stint in Vietnam, but he returned to gang life and helped guide the Mullens into a profitable alliance with Howie Winter of the Winter Hill Gang in Somerville. Nee was a player in the Irish mob wars (see "The Irish Mob Wars," page 120), as well as being an organizer of a major gun-smuggling operation that shipped weapons from the United States to the Irish Republican Army. In 1972, Nee participated in a key meeting with Whitey Bulger, Howie Winter, Tommy King and others at Chandler's Restaurant in the South End that attempted to end the violence. Nee served time in prison for weapons smuggling and an armored car robbery. He returned to Boston and, with Richard Farrell and Michael Blythe, wrote *A Criminal and an Irishman: The Inside Story of the Boston Mob–IRA Connection*, published in 2006.

# The Men in the Mob

## Raymond Loreto Salvatore Patriarca Sr.

*Nickname "The Man," "El Padrone"*
*Born: March 17, 1908*
*Died: July 7, 1984, North Providence, Rhode Island*
*Address: 168 Atwells Avenue, Providence, Rhode Island;*
*18 Golini Drive, Johnston, Rhode Island*
*Association: head of the Patriarca family*

Born on St. Patrick's Day 1908 to Italian immigrant parents in Worcester, Massachusetts, Raymond Loreto Salvatore Patriarca rose from his early days as a car-stealing, truck-hijacking, armed robber to become one of the most powerful mob bosses in the country.

Young Patriarca grew up with his family in Providence, Rhode Island, where his father operated a liquor store. When his dad died in 1925, the troubled teen quickly turned to a life of crime. By the late 1920s, he was hijacking trucks filled with booze and making money off prostitution. His arrest record when he reached the age of thirty included breaking and entering, bootlegging, safe cracking and white slavery. He also orchestrated a jailbreak that led to the death of a prison guard and trustee.

Smart and savvy, Patriarca gained a reputation for fairness that would later serve him well when he was asked to mediate disputes among warring Mafia factions. He could also be ruthless, a crime godfather who barked orders at underlings and made snap decisions on the life or death of some errant mob foot soldier. He's "just the toughest guy you ever saw," one Massachusetts State Police officer reportedly said in describing the mob boss, according to crime historian Allan May, who has written extensively on the American Mafia.

Growing up during the height of Prohibition, Patriarca quickly climbed the mob ladder to success, first as an associate and later as a member of the Mafia's New York faction. An arrest for a heist at a jewelry store in Brookline in 1938 enhanced his meteoric rise. He was sentenced to three to five years for armed robbery, carrying a gun without a permit and possession of burglary tools, but less than three months later, he was back on the street, released on a pardon by Massachusetts governor Charles F. Hurley. The swiftness with which Patriarca returned to his old haunts earned him new respect from other mobsters, now in awe of what they perceived as his "political connections." His release, however, also triggered a three-year investigation that led to the 1941 impeachment of a member of the Massachusetts Governor's Council, according to author Jack Beatty's landmark book on Boston mayor James

Michael Curley, *The Rascal King*. Daniel Coakley, a friend of Hurley's, got caught up in the scandal when it was discovered that he wrote letters to the parole board praising Patriarca's character, signing each with the fictitious name "Father Fagin," Beatty writes.

Newly freed from prison, Patriarca returned to Providence, where his power and influence soon made him a commanding force in the New England family that would later bear his name. By the time the 1950s rolled around, Patriarca was among the top crime figures in New England's underworld.

His ascent to the higher echelons of La Cosa Nostra was perhaps helped by his lack of rivals. His only Providence rival was rubbed out under Patriarca's orders in 1952. Irishman Carlton O'Brien was a former bootlegger who had moved into gambling before he was shot to death by Patriarca's men. That murder put the mob kingpin on the fast track to becoming the successor of Providence mob boss Phillip Bruccola. Two years later, in 1954, when Bruccola fled to his native Sicily to avoid prosecution on tax evasion charges, Patriarca ascended to the throne as head of the mob's New England branch.

With Patriarca instilled as the boss of New England, Providence became the epicenter of family operations. It was from here that Patriarca would rule for more than thirty years over a crime kingdom stretching from Connecticut to Maine. Father to the Patriarca crime family that still bears his name, he dominated the region's rackets with a control that was unmatched by any of his mob peers. His reign was ruthless and brutal, marked by a string of bloody mob hits.

In the late 1950s, he began a close association with a small-time runner for Boston bookies who reportedly was being shaken down regularly by other mobsters. Hoping to solve that problem, Gennaro Angiulo approached Patriarca and offered him $50,000, promising the mob boss an additional $100,000 annually from bookmaking proceeds in Boston in exchange for some protection against the bullies. The arrangement elevated Angiulo to the status of a made man, even though he had never murdered anyone, and kept money flowing into Patriarca's pockets.

By February 1961, however, Patriarca was under scrutiny by U.S. attorney general Robert F. Kennedy, who targeted Patriarca and thirty-nine other top racketeers for investigation and prosecution. That same year, FBI director J. Edgar Hoover named Patriarca as "Boston's Top Hoodlum" and said he was among the members of a "commission" of top organized crime leaders who had a controlling influence on the nation's rackets, a congressional investigation into the mob found.

In March of the following year, Hoover had listening devices installed in Patriarca's Coin-O-Matic Distributing Company, a vending machine and pinball business located at 168 Atwells Avenue in the predominantly Italian section of Providence known as Federal Hill. According to *The Underboss* by Dick Lehr and Gerard O'Neill, Patriarca controlled the mob's loan-sharking, gambling and pornography interests in New England from his Atwells Avenue office, along with his hidden interest in two Las Vegas casinos and deals in Florida and Philadelphia. He also collected payments from people involved in truck hijackings and drug trafficking, but he forbade his own men to get involved in the narcotics trade.

The bugs planted by Hoover's men in 1962 would reveal even more about Patriarca's organization, which had by now forged ties with the Genovese and Profaci/Colombo crime families in New York. During the three years the electronic bugs were in place, authorities recorded talks of political payoffs to legislators, judges and even officials in the governor's office in both Rhode Island and Massachusetts, along with discussions of gambling debts and collections. And, of course, there were mentions of murders.

"In this thing of ours, your love for your mother and father is one thing. Your love for 'the family' is a different kind of love," Patriarca is overheard telling an associate in one bugged conversation. In another, an enraged Patriarca and his underboss, Angiulo, are heard discussing hit men Joseph "The Animal" Barboza, Vincent "Jimmy" Flemmi (the brother of Stephen Flemmi) and another mob associate who had ordered the two gunmen to make a hit without Patriarca's knowledge.

"Patriarca told Angiulo that he explained to Flemmi…that no more killings were to take place unless he, Patriarca, cleared him," a memo to FBI head J. Edgar Hoover notes. "Jerry [Angiulo] also explained that he also had a talk with Flemmi. He pointed out that Patriarca had a high regard for Flemmi but that he thought that Flemmi did not use sufficient common sense when it came to killing people. Angiulo gave Flemmi a lecture on killing people, pointing out that he should not kill people because he had an argument…If an argument does ensue, he should leave and get word to Raymond Patriarca who, in turn, will either 'OK' or deny the 'hit' on this individual, depending on the circumstances," the memo, released as part of a congressional probe, states.

In July 1965, the FBI stopped electronic monitoring of Patriarca's office under orders from President Lyndon B. Johnson, who told the public he was opposed to obtaining evidence through electronic eavesdropping, an investigative report compiled for Congress shows. In the end, the information obtained during three years of illegal wiretaps was all for nothing. Because investigators never took out a warrant to install those devices, the information gathered against Patriarca and his family could never be used to prosecute him. Instead, authorities were forced to look for other means to put him behind bars.

That opportunity came in the form of a burley Portuguese hit man nicknamed "The Animal." Joseph Barboza hated snitches. He never really wanted to rat out his pals. But then FBI special agents Dennis Condon and H. Paul Rico began courting him, hoping he would become a government witness. It wasn't long before the two agents convinced Barboza he was on the mob's hit list, especially after "The Animal's" friends began turning up dead around Boston.

Soon, the hit man, described in FBI memos as "a professional assassin" considered by law enforcement to be "the most dangerous person known," was working with the feds. In 1967, Barboza's testimony put Patriarca and Enrico Tameleo, a longtime underboss, behind bars for ten years on a conspiracy to murder charge in connection with the slaying of Providence bookmaker Willie Marfeo. After only five years in prison, Patriarca was freed in 1974 and resumed control of Providence's criminal organization. Less than two years later, on February 11, 1976, Barboza was dead, killed by four shotgun blasts to the chest as he walked to his car in San Francisco (see "Joseph Barboza," page 34).

Patriarca's legal problems were far from over. In 1978, mobster Vincent Teresa testified that Patriarca was present when the CIA handed out a $4 million murder contract to the mob with the instructions that they were to kill Cuban leader Fidel Castro. Teresa claimed Patriarca helped pick a Brookline, Massachusetts convict by the name of Maurice Werner to kill Castro, but the assassination plot was later scrapped.

In 1983, Patriarca was again facing charges for ordering the murder of Raymond "Baby" Curcio in 1965 after Curcio and Teresa burglarized the home of Patriarca's brother Joseph. Four months later, in March 1984, Patriarca was arrested again, this time as he lay in a hospital bed, for ordering the 1968 killing of Robert Candos, a bank robber whom Patriarca believed was going to take the stand against him.

Patriarca never got the chance to defend himself in court on either case because on July 11, 1984, he was rushed from the home of his nightclub hostess girlfriend to a Rhode Island hospital, where the seventy-six-year-old died from a massive heart attack later that day.

Under indictment for two murders at the time of his death, Patriarca's demise left the mob's New England faction weak and in disarray. By the time Patriarca's son Raymond "Junior" Patriarca Jr. assumed command, organized crime in New England had taken a major hit.

# RAYMOND J. PATRIARCA

*Nicknames: "Junior," "Rubber Lips"*
*Born: February 24, 1945*
*Address: Lincoln, Rhode Island*
*Affiliations: Patriarca family, Genovese/Gambino families of New York*

It was supposed to be done in complete secrecy: this ceremony that inducted four men into an association that its bosses would swear didn't exist. "I enter alive into this organization and leave it dead," the men intoned after blood was drawn from each one's finger and a holy card with an image of a saint was burned. A throng of New England mobsters watched as the four were made into La Cosa Nostra. They swore to "enter into this organization to protect my family and to protect all my friends I swear not to divulge this secret and to obey with love and omerta."

Unfortunately for "omerta" (silence), federal agents were listening in, tipped off that an induction ceremony would be held at the Medford, Massachusetts, home on Guild Street on October 29, 1989. The five-hour tape of the ceremony proved that, despite protestations to the contrary by groups like the Italian-American Civil Rights League, the Mafia was an actual organization, with rules that verged on religious doctrine.

Blame for this major slip in protocol was laid primarily at the doorstep of the man who had succeeded his father as Mafia crime boss, a scion who was considered just a dim cutout of his more ruthless father. Raymond J. Patriarca, known as Junior, was the son of Raymond Loreto Salvatore Patriarca Sr., who had led the Italian faction of the mob from Rhode Island until his death in 1984. After a power struggle among his son, Gennaro Angiulo of the North End, Boston enforcer Ilario Zannino and others, Junior emerged as boss. New York crime families had a hand in settling the matter.

Many mob watchers considered the thirty-nine-year-old an odd choice. (A better choice, *Boston Globe* scribe Kevin Cullen wrote in 1990, would have been tough guy Nicholas "Nicky" Bianco, a pal of Francis "Cadillac Frank" Salemme and a former New Yorker.) While his father had grown up poor and never finished high school, Junior grew up in an affluent Providence, Rhode Island suburb and attended (but did not graduate from) college.

One unnamed source told Christopher Callahan of the Associated Press in July 1985, "This kid still's got milk on his face." He was also visible in the community, a Mafioso no-no, Callahan reported. This included lending office space to the Italian-American Civil Rights League, headed by the soon-to-be whacked Joseph Colombo, and investing in a Rhode Island eatery that featured giant photos of 1930s gangsters. He also regularly called in to Rhode Island radio talk shows.

Four years later, Junior made the ultimate gaffe by authorizing an induction ceremony that was, unbeknownst to him at the time, recorded by the feds. Included among those present at the Medford ceremony, according to reports in March 1990 when the taping was made public, were Joseph "J.R." Russo, Vincent M. "The Animal" Ferrara, Robert F. Carrozza, Matthew Guglielmetti, Charles Quintina and Angelo "Sonny" Mercurio. Inducted were Robert P. Deluca, Richard J.E. Floramo, Carmen A. Tortora and Vincent Federico, who hosted the event at his sister's home. Capo Biagio DiGiacomo allegedly presided over the ceremony, translating the Italian for the participants.

In March 1990, Junior Patriarca was indicted on a host of racketeering charges. In December 1991, he pleaded guilty and was sentenced to eight years in prison. While he served his sentence, boss duties were assumed by Salemme. Bianco, a member of the Colombo crime family, was indicted in 1990 on a slew of charges, including conspiracy to murder, wire fraud and interstate travel in aid of racketeering. He was stricken with Lou Gehrig's disease and died in prison in 1994. In 1998, Junior was released from prison, and reportedly he has retired from mob activity.

## ALEXANDER F. PETRICONE JR.

*Stage name: Alex Rocco*
*Nicknames: "Bobo," "Bo"*
*Born: February 29, 1936, Cambridge*
*Address: Jacques Street, Somerville, before moving to California in 1963*
*Affiliation: Winter Hill Gang*

Once a gangster does not mean always a gangster. For proof, you only have to look at the career of Alexander F. Petricone, a player on the fringes of the Winter Hill Gang who quickly realized that life in the mob can be nasty, brutish and short. As actor Alex Rocco, Petricone was

# The Men in the Mob

The scene could be a still from a movie with actor Alex Rocco, who specializes in playing "heavies." In reality, the image above is a November 1, 1961 newspaper photo of Alexander "Bobo" Petricone (the actor's real name), who was arrested in connection with the October 31 slaying in Charlestown of racketeer Bernard McLaughlin. Petricone was not charged with the crime, and he soon left for California, where he had a long and fruitful acting career, with stints in *The Godfather* and *The Friends of Eddie Coyle*. *Courtesy of the Boston Public Library, Print Department.*

able to parlay his insider knowledge into a series of memorable screen appearances in a storyline that could have been written by mystery scribe Elmore Leonard.

As a bartender and resident of the Winter Hill area of Somerville, Petricone was friendly with the guys in the rackets. According to Vincent Teresa in his book *My Life in the Mob*, George McLaughlin tried to pick up Petricone's girlfriend in September 1961, a precipitating incident in Boston's bloody gang wars in the early 1960s. Twenty-five-year-old Petricone was arrested with James J. "Buddy" McLean of Somerville in connection with the noontime slaying of Bernard McLaughlin, George's brother, in Charlestown on October 31 but was later released from custody with no charges filed (see "The Irish Mob Wars," page 120).

Petricone wisely left for California, where a friend told the heavy-set former bartender that he should try acting due to his "interesting" face, as Petricone told a *Boston Globe* reporter in 1975. With coaching from actor Leonard Nimoy (a native of Boston's West End), he toned down his Boston accent, and wise guy wannabe Petricone became actor Alex Rocco, who talked his way onto a one-line stint on the TV show *Batman*. Other roles followed on TV and in the movies, including one as a bank robber in *The Friends of Eddie Coyle* (see "*The Friends of Eddie Coyle*," page 138). Perhaps his most memorable role was as Las Vegas gangster Moe Green, who gets shot in the eye in *The Godfather*. He eventually branched out to portray a variety of characters, including a reoccurring spot on TV's *The Simpsons*. In 1989, he won an Emmy for his role in the short-lived series *The Famous Teddy Z*. He also poked fun at the bloody horse head scene in *The Godfather* in an edgy Audi commercial aired during the 2008 Super Bowl, in which he wakes covered with oil to find an Audi bumper in his bed.

Given the trail of murders and broken lives left by the Winter Hill Gang, Petricone made a smart career move in 1963. His success also underscores the blurring between hype and reality in Boston's underworld.

# H. PAUL RICO

*Born: April 29, 1925, Belmont, Massachusetts*
*Died: January 14, 2004, Tulsa, Oklahoma*
*Address: Miami Shores, Florida*
*Affiliation: FBI*

# The Men in the Mob

What motivates a mobster to turn on his comrades in crime and become an informer? It's an issue law enforcers have long pondered in their efforts to build cases against criminals. But here's another question: what motivates a FBI agent to reject everything he learned as a lawman and side with the underworld?

By dying in a medical bed at age seventy-eight, retired FBI agent H. Paul Rico avoided having to answer that question—and many more—in a court of law. Rico was then under indictment for providing information to Stephen "The Rifleman" Flemmi and James "Whitey" Bulger for a hit on a prominent Tulsa businessman who stood in the Boston mobsters' way. The indictment was only part of the story of Rico. It turns out that the FBI agent had been looking the other way for years as the bodies piled up in Boston's turf wars at the hands of the men he was using as informants.

Born in a wealthy suburb outside Boston, Rico graduated from Boston College and was assigned to the Boston bureau of the FBI in the 1960s. He established a reputation as a tenacious agent with an insider's knowledge of mob organizations. He was one of the agents who worked to turn Joseph "The Animal" Barboza into an informant, as well as recruit Irish mobsters to snitch on Italian gangsters. He reputedly knew just how to set one mobster against another. To be sure, in this kind of work the line blurs between right and wrong, but along the way in his twenty-five-year FBI career, Rico passed a no-return mark into amorality.

He and the FBI have been accused of knowing through wiretaps beforehand of a planned hit on small-time mobster Edward "Teddy" Deegan, who was shot in Chelsea, Massachusetts, in March 1965. Not only did the FBI fail to step in to prevent the murder, but Rico stayed silent when four men who did not commit that crime went to jail for it. Joseph Salvati, Peter J. Limone, Louis Greco and Henry Tameleo were convicted in 1968 of Deegan's murder, based on the testimony of Barboza, who admitted his part in the slaying. Greco and Tameleo died in prison, while Salvati's sentence was commuted in 1997 amid doubts about his guilt after decades of pressure by attorney Victor Garo. Limone's conviction was tossed out in January 2001. Evidence finally revealed that Deegan's real killers were Barboza and Vincent "Jimmy the Bear" Flemmi, brother of Stephen Flemmi, who sought to eliminate mob rivals. Barboza fingered Salvati and Greco because he had had run-ins with them. Jimmy Flemmi, like his brother, was an FBI informant.

In another mindboggling development, Francis "Cadillac Frank" Salemme testified in 2003 that in 1965, Agent Rico had provided him with information on the whereabouts of rival Edward "Punchy" McLaughlin, leading to McLaughlin's slaying at a West Roxbury bus stop (see "The Irish Mob Wars," page 120).

That Rico had few qualms about what he had done became apparent in May 2001, when he was called before a congressional committee investigating the use of informants by the FBI. Connecticut representative Christopher Shays pressed Rico on whether he felt any remorse for allowing an innocent man like Salvati to go to jail. "Remorse for what?" Rico rejoined, according to news reports. "Would you like tears or something?"

Two years later, the depth of Rico's lack of conscience was further exposed. Rico had retired from the FBI in 1975, and by 1981, he was chief of security for World Jai Alai, a sporting company owned by Roger M. Wheeler, the chairman of Telex Corp. When Wheeler grew suspicious that mob interests led by Stephen Flemmi and Whitey Bulger were skimming profits from World Jai Alai, the fifty-five-year-old businessman was shot in the head in 1981 by John Martorano on orders from Bulger and Flemmi. Rico allegedly provided Martorano with a physical description of Wheeler, his home address and the make and license number of his car. It took years for law enforcement to catch up to Rico, and then only after Flemmi started talking and Bulger went on the lam. On October 9, 2003, Rico, living near Miami, Florida, was arrested and charged in connection with Wheeler's murder (see "The Jai Alai Killings," page 125).

But Rico outwitted the wheels of justice. On January 14, 2004, while awaiting trial, he died in a medical unit at David L. Moss Criminal Justice Center in Tulsa. Wheeler's family were denied the chance to confront the man who cold-bloodedly arranged for Wheeler's death, and the public was denied the chance to learn just what makes a lawman abandon everything he had sworn to protect.

Limone, Salvati and the families of the men wrongly convicted of the Deegan murder filed suit against the government and, in 2007, were awarded sums totaling $101.75 million. That the four were "not choir boys," as a reporter put it, was beside the point. They were innocent of the murder they were accused of committing.

# Joseph Russo

*Nickname: "J.R."*
*Address: Guild Street, Medford*
*Born: 1931, East Boston*
*Died: June 1998, Springfield, Missouri*
*Affiliation: Patriarca family, Lucchese family*

He was dubbed "a genius with a carbine" by fellow mobster Ilario Zannino for the way he gunned down hit-man-turned-stool pigeon Joseph "The Animal" Barboza, but it wasn't just his killing skills that made Joseph "J.R." Russo memorable. It was the way he conducted part of a now not-so-secret Mafia ritual.

A mob capo known for his custom-made long-collar shirts and his sharp features, Russo tracked Barboza to San Francisco, where he cut down the FBI informant with four close-range shotgun blasts on February 11, 1976 (see "Joseph Barboza," page 34). The murder of the burley Barboza was enough to win Russo notoriety among his mob peers, but it was his raspy voice on an FBI tape of a mob induction ceremony that made him infamous.

The site of the October 29, 1989 ceremony was an ordinary yellow house in Medford that was home to the sister of Vincent Federico, one of four men scheduled to become made men in the Patriarca crime family. Captured for

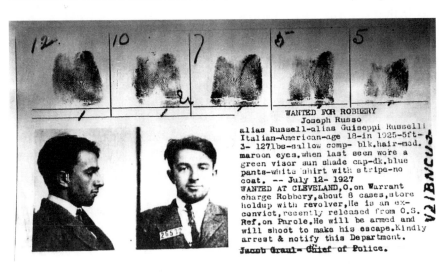

Police posters of Joseph "J.R." Russo. *Courtesy of the Boston Public Library, Print Department.*

A 1952 photo of Joseph "J.R." Russo, a consigliere in the Boston mob. *Courtesy of the Boston Public Library, Print Department.*

posterity, Russo is heard issuing La Cosa Nostra's sacred oath of "omerta," or silence, to the four new members. It was at this same ceremony that Russo would be named head of the Boston faction, replacing Gennaro Angiulo, who was behind bars on racketeering charges (see "Gennaro Angiulo," page 25).

Listening, as the men pricked their trigger fingers to draw blood and burned holy cards of the Patriarca family saint, was a team of FBI agents who were building a case against the mob. Six months after that ceremony, twenty mob members, including Patriarca family head Raymond Patriarca Jr. and Russo, would be under indictment on charges that included racketeering, gambling, extortion, drug trafficking and murder. Russo later died in a federal prison in Springfield, Missouri, where he was serving eighteen years for Barboza's murder.

## FRANCIS P. SALEMME

*Nickname: "Cadillac Frank"*
*Alias: Julian Daniel Selig*
*Born: August 18, 1933, Boston*
*Association: Patriarca family, Winter Hill Gang*

In the end, there was no Cadillac for the man known as "Cadillac Frank" Salemme.

The mob hit man who rose through the ranks to become head of the Patriarca crime family, only to turn snitch against fellow mobsters and the FBI, got a new name, a new address and $5,000 toward a used car when he entered the federal Witness Protection Program in 2003. The money was hardly enough to buy the kind of flashy Cadillacs Salemme loved to drive.

Yet it was more than his mob rivals planned to give him. They had already picked out a round of bullets as a going-away present when they shot up his

# The Men in the Mob

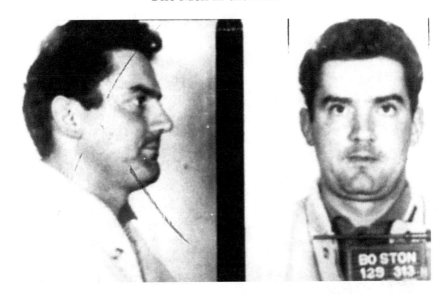

*Above*: Mug shot of Frances P. "Cadillac Frank" Salemme from 1969. *Courtesy of the Boston Public Library, Print Department.*

*Below*: In this photo dated June 27, 1949, two alleged safecrackers were taken into Cambridge police headquarters following their capture after attempting to jump out of a second-story window at the International Printers Ink Building, 175 Albany Street. *Left to right*: suspect Frank Salemme of Somerville, Officer Roy Hughes, suspect Alexander Vailliant and Officer Charles J. Cogan. Salemme would go on to be one of Boston's most prominent and dangerous mobsters. *Courtesy of the Boston Public Library.*

Francis "Cadillac Frank" Salemme in 1995.
*Courtesy of the Boston Police Department.*

black BMW in the parking lot of a Saugus, Massachusetts pancake house on June 16, 1989, leaving him seriously wounded. Salemme had a briefcase containing $12,000 in cash with him when he arrived at the International House of Pancakes. As he stepped out of his car, he was shot in the chest and leg by a gunman who had been following in a car close behind. Salemme reportedly ran into the restaurant's lobby but quickly ran back out, supposedly to keep others from becoming targets. As he did so, he was hit once again. Taken to AtlantiCare Medical Hospital in nearby Lynn, Massachusetts, he was protected by armed state troopers while he recovered.

The same day Salemme was shot, William P. Grasso, an underboss known as "The Wild Man," was found dead along the banks of the Connecticut River with a bullet in his head. Police initially called it a coincidence. It wasn't. According to mob historian Allan May, the dual attacks were orchestrated by a renegade faction of the Boston family under the leadership of new family consigliere Joseph "J.R." Russo, his stepbrother Robert F. "Bobby Russo" Carrozza and Vincent "Vinnie the Animal" Ferrara, both capos. Russo, whose status in the mob was elevated after he killed informant Joseph Barboza in 1979, was attempting to seize control of Boston's gambling and extortion action. The gang war that resulted from the takeover would leave more than a dozen dead before it finally ended in 1994.

Salemme should have been used to all that infighting. Raised in the Jamaica Plain neighborhood of Boston, he became a loyal mob soldier early on in life and would later achieve the dubious distinction of being the first Boston man to head up Italian Mafia factions in both the North End and Rhode Island. In the early 1960s, he participated in Boston's Irish mob wars by murdering numerous rivals in nearby Charlestown. In 2003, he testified before Congress about those killings. "The Hugheses, the McLaughlins, they were all eliminated, and I was a participant in just about all of them, planned them and did them," he told congressional investigators in 2003.

Yet it wasn't that murder spree that garnered the attention of his underworld peers. It was the 1965 attempted murder of John E. Fitzgerald, the attorney for mobster-turned-informant Joseph Barboza. Hoping to persuade Barboza to back out of an agreement with prosecutors to testify against mob boss Raymond Patriarca Sr., Salemme and Flemmi arranged for a bomb to be planted under the hood of Fitzgerald's car, a black Oldsmobile given to him by Barboza in lieu of payment for legal services. The bomb took off Fitzgerald's leg and damaged windows in nearby apartments but did little to stop Barboza's testimony. With the heat on, Salemme went into hiding, where he remained until 1972, when he was captured by FBI agent John Connolly while walking along a street in Manhattan.

Salemme did seventeen years in prison for that crime, receiving special recognition not once but twice while incarcerated for rescuing a guard who was shot by an inmate and for helping to quell several prison disturbances. Meanwhile, Flemmi, his colleague in the car bombing, fled to Montreal, returning to Boston in 1974 only after all charges against him were dropped, a feat reportedly arranged by Connolly.

Soon after Salemme was released from prison in 1986, he saw an opportunity to refresh his friendship with the Patriarca family. With Gennaro Angiulo serving prison time on a racketeering charge, Salemme was looking to move up in the ranks. Russo and his rogue contingent, hoping to retain control of the rackets in Boston, organized the pancake house attack in a bid to stop him. The feud left at least ten dead. New York crime families brokered a deal among the warring factions that ended the bloodshed. Raymond J. "Junior" Patriarca, son of Patriarca Sr., was nominally in charge (with Russo and Nicholas Bianco as top lieutenants), but not for long; he was caught by an FBI bug presiding over a Mafia induction ceremony (see mob induction ceremony, pages 48, 58, 65, 71, 75). By 1991, Junior Patriarca and Bianco were in prison, and with the backing of Bulger and Flemmi, Salemme became the de facto boss of the Patriarca family in a move that for the first time in more than thirty years shifted the mob's power base from Providence to Boston. His reign would be short-lived, however. In early 1995, a grand jury handed up a thirty-seven-count indictment against Salemme and six others, including Bulger and Flemmi, charging them with racketeering. Bulger fled after being alerted to the pending indictments by now retired FBI agent John Connolly.

Salemme and Flemmi were arrested. The mob kingpin known as "Cadillac Frank" would later serve eleven years in federal prison on racketeering charges.

While incarcerated, the mobster learned that both Bulger and Flemmi had been working as informants and had fed information about him to the FBI. That revelation was a turning point for Salemme, who soon agreed to be a witness against his two former friends. His testimony would also help convict FBI agent John Connolly of corruption and other charges.

In exchange for helping the government, Salemme was released early from prison and placed in the federal Witness Protection Program. In 2004, he was arrested again, charged with lying to federal agents about the 1993 murder of nightclub owner Steve DiSarro. Prosecutors believed that Salemme's son, Frank Jr., strangled DiSarro and his father helped dispose of the body. Salemme, whose son died in 1995, denied any involvement in the murder. On July 16, 2008, however, the elder Salemme pleaded guilty to perjury and obstruction of justice in the case and was sentenced to five years in prison.

## CHARLES "KING" SOLOMON

*Aliases: Charles Simon, Charles Solomont, Carl Solomont*
*Born: 1884 or 1886, possibly in Russia*
*Died: January 24, 1933, Cotton Club, Boston*
*Addresses: Brookline, Massachusetts, and New York*
*Associations: Murder Inc., Lucky Luciano and his own extensive liquor, narcotics, theater and nightclub enterprises*

He was called "King" for a good reason—there was little in Boston in the 1920s and early 1930s that Charles Solomon didn't control or have a hand in, even while he managed to stay a step ahead of the law. He was the *über* boss of the Boston rackets, a Russian Jewish immigrant who made enough money to retire but couldn't give up the street life. From rumrunning to dope peddling to prostitution, from nightclubs to theaters, his was an empire both illegal and legit. His last words—recounted slightly differently depending on the reporter doing the telling—seem like a bad imitation of James Cagney. As a bootlegger, he devised elaborate schemes to deliver hooch to New Englanders and did deals with the Murder Inc. boys of New York. As a nightclub impresario, he hobnobbed with vaudeville stars of his day—Sally Rand, Sophie Tucker and Texas Guinan. His legacy has a particularly insidious footnote. He was the owner of the Cocoanut Grove nightclub from 1931 to 1933, and while he was long gone at the time of the infamous 1942

Charles "King" Solomon, at the far left, was one of Boston's most notorious Jewish gangsters in the Prohibition period. Solomon presided over a network of alcohol and drug dealing, all the while hobnobbing with singers and celebrities at his nightclub, the Cocoanut Grove. Here he is seated with his bandleader (left to right) Joe Solomon, Dorothy "Dot" England, his frequent companion, and club maitre d' Teddy Roy. *Courtesy of the Boston Public Library, Print Department.*

fire that killed nearly five hundred people, he had established a custom that would doom so many: he insisted on keeping the doors to the club locked both inside and out (see "Cocoanut Grove," page 98).

The man who would be king was born in Russia to Joseph and Sarah Blum Solomon and grew up in Salem, Massachusetts, after his parents immigrated to New England. He became a professional bondsman but soon branched out into other enterprises. His first arrest came in his teens, and he would go on to have twenty-one court records in the next twenty-one years. He was first nabbed in 1911 with Golda Solomon (likely a relative) for keeping a house of ill repute. His record includes breaking and entering, being idle and disorderly, receiving stolen goods, gambling, perjury and narcotics dealing. Each time he managed to get off with fines or short jail sentences.

Frustrated, police also nabbed him on a variety of small stuff: driving on the wrong side of Dover Street, making a wrong turn and "using profanity to a police officer in performance of his duty." Despite his legal battles, Solomon eventually commanded a fleet of boats guided by secret radio stations along the coast of New Jersey and Long Island that brought booze in from Central America. He bought at least three Boston theaters, several nightclubs, a beauty parlor and restaurants in outlying cities; he owned hotels in New York, a factory in Brooklyn and a nightclub in Montreal. He obtained the Cocoanut Grove nightclub in 1931 and used it as his personal showcase.

Austen Lake of the *Boston Evening American* describes "I Solomon Pax, Fecit," who "sat on his lobby throne, or with assorted society, and flashed his $500 store teeth, occasionally excusing himself at the discrete eye-wink of some private courtier to 'see a certain party about a certain matter which concerns you know what.'" While he hated publicity, he craved the limelight, and he cut a fine figure in evening clothes. His acquaintances ranged from fellow mobsters and showgirls to lawyers and politicians. Texas Guinan tartly called him the "Man with the Lascivious Lip" and "Old Slobber Puss," and he loved it, Lake asserted.

The exterior of the Cotton Club and the final nightcap for racketeer Charles "King" Solomon in 1933. *Courtesy of the Boston Public Library, Print Department.*

At age forty-nine, Solomon was at the height of his power, dubbed the "Capone of the East" by federal agents, according to the *Boston Globe*. "Capone had a 'mob,' Solomon had a machine that wanted no opposition and took care of opponents so efficiently that there was little that became news," the *Globe* reported. A police captain once asked Solomon, "Charlie, you've got millions. Why don't you get out of the racket?" The king waved him off, saying, "Don't be silly."

But even a king can't rule forever. On January 8, 1933, federal indictments were handed down fingering Solomon as the "brains" of a $14 million liquor-running enterprise that smuggled whiskey to the United States from Belize and St. Pierre. Arrested, Solomon posted the $5,000 bail and went about his business, likely figuring he would beat the rap as he did all others. "I have friends in high places," he told reporters. On the evening of January 23, two days before he was to appear in federal court, Solomon, as was his habit, spent the evening at the Cocoanut Grove. His wife, Bertha "Billie" Solomon, was likely at her home in Taunton. He was on the outs with his main squeeze, a looker named Dorothy England, so he was out to impress two young dancers. With $4,600 in his pocket, he, the girls and Joe Solomon, his bandleader (most sources say the two were not related), grabbed a taxi to the Cotton Club on Tremont Street, near Massachusetts Avenue, a club catering to Boston's African American community where a band continued to play. Solomon was friendly with owner Tommy Maren (Solomon might have been part owner of the Cotton Club), and the party was going strong about 3:30 a.m.

At one point, Solomon left his table to go to the bathroom and was followed by a group of men who had been drinking sullenly at a nearby table. Witnesses reported hearing an argument about a "double-crossing, no good rat," with Solomon saying something to the effect of, "You got my roll, now what do you want?" The reply: "You've had this coming for a long time." Shots rang out, the men fled and Solomon staggered out, shot four times in the chest, abdomen and neck. "The rats got me," he grunted before being rushed to the hospital, where he died. He was found to be missing the $4,600. (His last utterance has also been reported as: "The dirty rats got me," or, "Those dirty rats—got me.")

"Bullets sang the requiem of 'King' Solomon yesterday and wiped forever from his face the smile that thousands knew," the *Boston Globe* declared on January 25. That Solomon affected many is demonstrated by the throngs of onlookers who crowded Fuller Street in Brookline to watch as his hearse passed during his large funeral procession. Police arrested and questioned

*Above*: James "Skeets" Coyne was brought back from Michigan City, Indiana, for questioning in the Charles "King" Solomon murder. A large number of hoods were brought in for questioning on the case; Coyne was one of three convicted. *Courtesy of the Boston Public Library, Print Department.*

*Below*: The size of the crowd at King Solomon's funeral tells something about the impact he had in Boston. In this photo, crowds line Fuller Street in Brookline as his hearse passes to bid a final farewell to the notorious kingpin who presided over the popular Cocoanut Grove nightclub. *Courtesy of the Boston Public Library, Print Department.*

the men seen at the Cotton Club that night. Three were convicted. James J. "Skeets" Coyne and James J. Scully served time for manslaughter, and John F. O'Donnell was convicted of being an accessory after the fact.

While some news reports maintain the King met his end as the result of a "cheap holdout" by impulsive petty thieves who knew that Solomon always carried wads of cash, the *New York Times* quoted assistant U.S. attorney Leonard Greenstone as saying, "I believe Boston Charlie was put on the spot to seal his lips" about the rumrunning ring. Mob watchers speculate that the Italian mob in the North End ordered the hit to eliminate a rival. Reporter Austen Lake, however, maintains that Solomon skimmed too much off the top while safekeeping funds from a recent Fall River holdup and thus "carved his initials on the bullet that killed him." Coyle and Scully were not associated with any particular gangs, either Irish or Italian.

Solomon evaded the law even after death. Despite his reputed millions, his estate was valued at just $457.22, according to documents filed by his widow. Solomon's lawyer, Barnet "Barney" Welansky, emerged from obscurity to take over the Cocoanut Grove, and he, too, made it a habit to keep the doors of the nightclub locked inside and out.

## FRANK WALLACE

*Born: Unknown*
*Died: December 22, 1931, Boston*
*Address: Gustin Street, South Boston*
*Association: Gustin Gang*

Three Irish-American brothers—Frank, Steve and James Wallace—from the South Boston neighborhood known as Southie first came to the attention of authorities about 1910, when they began hijacking and looting delivery trucks while they were stopped at intersections. Originally known as the "Tailboard Thieves," the brothers, led by Frank, moved from hijackings to armed robbery and later, with the advent of Prohibition, into bootlegging. By the time the Roaring Twenties arrived, the trio had amassed a brisk hijacking and bootlegging business, along with a slew of criminal charges, including larceny, assault and battery and breaking and entering. With older brother Steve Wallace, a former boxer, serving as his enforcer, Frank and his crew—now known as the Gustin Gang in deference to the South Boston street where the Wallaces hung out—soon became one of the most powerful

*Left*: One of the earliest Irish gangs in Boston was named after this street in South Boston. The Gustin Gang was formed by Steve Wallace with his brothers Frank and Jimmy Wallace in the 1920s for bootlegging and other less-than-legal enterprises. *Courtesy of the Boston Public Library, Leslie Jones Collection.*

*Below*: A mug shot of Frank Wallace, a member of the Gustin Gang. Wallace and one of his henchmen were killed in a shootout with an Italian gang led by mobster Joseph Lombardo in a dispute over the bootlegging business. The shooting on Hanover Street in Boston's North End occurred as veterans packed Christmas baskets for the poor just one flight above the gunplay three days before Christmas in 1931. *Courtesy of the Boston Public Library, Print Department.*

and well-organized criminal enterprises in Prohibition-era Boston. Flashing fake badges, they quickly took over much of Southie's thriving booze business by impersonating Prohibition agents and confiscating beer shipments from rival bootleggers. They would then sell the confiscated beer to speakeasies, delivering it to customers themselves.

Frank's reputation as a street tough was solidified when he was charged with robbery and murder in Michigan following a $14,000 heist at the *Detroit News* that left one person dead. He was acquitted in that case and returned to Boston, where, given Frank's political connections, some suspect he may have gotten away with more than just selling a few cases of illegal home brew. In fact, despite their criminal proclivities, all three brothers escaped with few convictions on their records and even less jail time. Whether it was kismet or close political ties, the Wallace boys seemed blessed by fate.

Then, three days before Christmas 1931, the gang's luck ran out. Touched by a wintry chill blowing in off the cold Atlantic, December 21, 1931, marked a watershed in Boston mob history. By the end of that day, the Gustin Gang no longer ruled the city's streets. The Italian Mafia had established a foothold. The tipping point came during a meeting between Frank Wallace and Italian mobster Joseph Lombardo. The two groups had been feuding for about a week, police would later say, after the Gustin Gang hijacked a truck filled with $50,000 in liquor and hid it in the Nantasket summer home of a Harvard Medical School doctor.

Wallace expected a showdown when he walked into the Testa Building in Boston's predominantly Italian North End that chilly winter day. Accompanied by enforcers Barney "Dodo" Walsh and Timothy Coffey, the Gustin boss showed up at Lombardo's C&F Importing Company at 317 Hanover Street with guns loaded. He was ready for trouble.

As war veterans packed Christmas baskets for the poor on the floor above, the three Gustin gangsters knocked on the door to Lombardo's third-floor office when a blaze of gunshots rang out. In the exchange of bullets, Wallace and Walsh were killed. Coffey ran down the hall and hid in an attorney's office until the police arrived. Seven guns were later found at the scene of the murders, but no one was ever charged. The ambush was later to become among the most infamous mob hits in Boston's crime history.

With Wallace now out of the picture, Lombardo's status in the Mafia got a huge boost. It also allowed the Italians to establish themselves as a dominant criminal organization in the city for more than fifty years.

# STEVE WALLACE

*Born: 1901*
*Died: unknown*
*Address: Gustin Street, South Boston*
*Association: Gustin Gang*

With the death of his brother Frank in a 1931 ambush in Boston's North End, Steve Wallace became head of the Gustin Gang, but the group's power waned following the shootout, never to recover. By 1933, the thirty-two-year-old gangster was wanted on an attempted murder charge for allegedly assaulting a Boston police detective and murdering the state's star witness. In June, Boston investigators tracked him to New York City, where, dressed in a natty brown suit and with $100 in his pocket, he was arrested while walking down Broadway.

Yet the luck that had come so easily to Wallace and his brothers in the past seemed to still be with him. Despite the charges against him, Steve Wallace would walk free yet again.

Frank Wallace's brother Steve Wallace (center), who took over the Gustin Gang following his brother's death, is flanked by authorities in a photo dated October 29, 1934. *Courtesy of the Boston Public Library, Print Department.*

Two years to the day of his brother's December 21, 1931 slaying, he was acquitted of assault with intent to murder the Boston detective. He promptly left the courthouse following that acquittal and quickly vanished. One year later, the diminutive mobster was being sought nationwide again, this time on a charge of conspiracy to murder the same police officer. On October 30, 1934, Wallace surrendered to detectives in South Boston. Few records of that case's outcome exist today, but by the late 1930s, both Steve Wallace and the Gustin Gang had vanished into obscurity.

## KEVIN WEEKS

*Nickname: "Two Weeks," "Kevin Squeeks"*
*Address: 8 Pilsduski Way, Old Colony Housing Project, South Boston;*
*Quincy Shore Drive, Quincy, Massachusetts*
*Born: March 21, 1956, South Boston, Massachusetts*
*Association: Winter Hill Gang*

In crime's netherworld of snitches, hit men and turncoats, no one was closer to Boston mob kingpin "Whitey" Bulger than Kevin Weeks, who called Bulger "Jimmy." Yet in the end, even he would rat out the legendary crime boss, implicating Bulger in at least six murders and taking down the FBI agent who became Bulger's friend.

Weeks's early life, however, was somewhat routine, filled with the things that most young boys enjoy. He was on his high school swim team, was taught how to box by his father and enjoyed hanging out on street corners with his pals, much like any kid reared in South Boston in the 1950s and 1960s.

Born to Margaret and John Weeks on March 21, 1956, Kevin Weeks was the fifth of six children raised by working-class parents at 8 Pilsduski Way in South Boston's Old Colony Housing Project, the same cluster of red brick tenements where FBI agent John Connolly lived as a child. Weeks's father, who trained prizefighters to bring in extra money, taught his three sons how to box but also encouraged them to do their best in school, perhaps seeing education as a way out of their dire life in public housing. Two of the boys would later graduate from Harvard University. The other, Kevin, would only make it through secondary school, graduating in 1974 from South Boston High School amid the turmoil of forced busing and desegregation. In 1976, Weeks took a job as a bouncer at Triple O's bar on Broadway in South Boston. It was a decision that would change his life.

*Above*: A surveillance photo taken by investigators showing Whitey Bulger walking with Stephen Flemmi on the left and Kevin Weeks on the right. The three would meet regularly late in the afternoon to walk around Castle Island in South Boston and talk business. *U.S. Drug Enforcement Agency file photo*.

*Left*: The West Fourth Street condo in South Boston purchased by Kevin Weeks is located next door to the home of his mentor, James "Whitey" Bulger. Bulger's condo is on the right. *Photo by Beverly Ford*.

# The Men in the Mob

Located a short walk from a subway station, the neighborhood bar was a popular hangout for members of the Winter Hill Gang, including gang leader James "Whitey" Bulger and his sidekick, Stephen Flemmi. Within two years, Weeks began working part time as Bulger's enforcer and driver. On the side, Weeks started his own loan-sharking operation, paying a portion of the proceeds to Bulger in tribute. By 1982, Weeks had quit his bouncer job to become a full-time mobster.

It didn't take him long to get involved in murder. On May 11, 1982, Weeks was staking out Anthony's Pier 4 restaurant on the South Boston waterfront under Bulger's orders, awaiting the appearance of former associate turned snitch Edward Brian Halloran, who was having dinner with a construction worker pal, Michael Donahue. As the two men drove out of the parking lot, Weeks radioed Bulger using the code "The balloon is in the air," a reference to Halloran's nickname, "Balloonhead." Within seconds, Bulger, wearing a brown Afro wig and mustache and carrying a .30-caliber carbine, drove his souped-up blue Chevrolet to the parking lot, along with a masked man armed with a Mac 10 and a silencer. After Bulger called out Halloran's name, the pair opened fire. A fuselage of bullets killed Donahue instantly and left Halloran, the father of two, clinging to life long enough to identify one of his assailants as James Flynn, a Winter Hill associate. Flynn, who was tried and acquitted for the murders, remained a suspect for seventeen years until 1999, when Weeks, cooperating with investigators, identified the killer as Bulger. The second murderer, who was wearing a mask at the time, has never been identified (see "Brian Halloran," page 119).

By the early 1980s, Weeks, described as "a surrogate son" to Bulger (although he would later cast their relationship as businessmen), was working as an enforcer for the Winter Hill crew, collecting loans and bets from local businessmen and receiving tribute from loan sharks and bookmakers. Soon, Bulger and Flemmi expanded their business into drug trafficking, with Weeks once again as enforcer. According to Weeks's memoir, *Brutal: The Untold Story of My Life Inside Whitey Bulger's Irish Mob*, Bulger began calling in drug dealers from throughout the Boston area for meetings, at which he would tell them that he had been offered a contract on their life. He would then demand a large payoff not to kill them.

"Jimmy, Stevie and I weren't in the import business and weren't bringing in the marijuana or the cocaine. We were in the shakedown business," Weeks would later write. "We didn't bring drugs in; we took money off the people who did. We never dealt with the street dealers, but rather with a dozen large-scale drug distributors all over the State who were bringing in the coke and marijuana and paying hundreds of thousands to Jimmy."

In 1995, after Bulger was indicted and had disappeared thanks to a tip from his FBI handler, Weeks began running the Winter Hill Gang, taking orders from the fugitive by phone and often meeting him at clandestine locations outside of Massachusetts. He also channeled thousands of dollars to his mentor, who reportedly stashed the loot in safety deposit boxes across the country.

By the late 1990s, there were whispers that "Whitey" was working as an informant for the feds. Then, in 1997, the *Boston Globe* disclosed that Bulger and Flemmi had met several times with now retired FBI agent John Connolly. Weeks said shortly after that article appeared he sat down with Connolly, who showed Weeks a copy of Bulger's FBI informant file. "The Mafia was going against Jimmy and Stevie, so Jimmy and Stevie went against them," he remembered Connolly saying, as if explaining the pair's cooperation.

Two years later, on November 17, 1999, Weeks and other members of the Winter Hill Gang were arrested in South Boston by federal Drug Enforcement Agents and the Massachusetts State Police and charged with a twenty-nine-count indictment under the Racketeer Influence and Corruption Act, commonly known as RICO. Stunned by the charges, Weeks refused to cooperate. But after cooling his heels in the federal penitentiary in Rhode Island for two weeks, the mobster had a change of heart. He decided to cooperate with investigators. That decision would earn him the nicknames "Two Weeks" and "Kevin Squeeks" on the streets of Southie.

Weeks claims the turning point came when he was approached by another prisoner, a member of the Patriarca family, who said, "Kid, what are you doing? Are you going to take it up the ass for these guys? Remember you can't rat on a rat. Those guys have been giving up everyone for thirty years." That conversation, along with a decision by hit man John Martorano to turn informant, prompted Weeks to cooperate.

Once he started talking, Weeks couldn't stop. He led investigators to the bodies of eight murder victims buried in and around Boston and agreed to testify against Bulger, Flemmi and Connolly in exchange for a five-year prison sentence.

Today, free from jail, Weeks has written two books about his mob exploits with coauthor Phyllis Karas. In addition to *Brutal*, he and Karas also penned *Where's Whitey*, which speculated about Bulger's life on the lam. Just days after that book was released, Bulger was arrested by federal agents at the Santa Monica, California apartment he shared with his longtime girlfriend, Catherine Greig.

## Howard Thomas Winter

*Nickname: "Howie"*
*Born: March 17, 1929, West Roxbury*
*Addresses: Charlestown, West Roxbury, Somerville*
*Affiliation: Winter Hill Gang*

Born on St. Patrick's Day, Howard "Howie" Winter, of both Irish and Italian ancestry, was a tough guy who, nonetheless, was known for being able to mediate among warring mob factions. It was just coincidence that he shared his name with the gang that he came to run in Somerville.

Founded by Buddy McLean, the Winter Hill Gang derived its name from Winter Hill in the Boston suburb of Somerville. It was taken over by Howie Winter after McLean's murder in 1966 during the Irish mob wars (see "The Irish Mob Wars," page 120). The conflict pitted Irish American gangsters in South Boston, Charlestown and Somerville against one another in a bloody battle for control of the Boston-area rackets.

When it came to fixing horse races, the Winter Hill Gang was one of the best. Led by Winter, the gang fixed races at scores of tracks along the East Coast, cashing in on winning horses to bring home big bundles of cash. The horse racing eventually brought in money to fuel other operations. It would also bring down the gang. By 1979, Winter and the rest of his Somerville crew were sent to prison for a $40 million scheme to fix races throughout New England. This time, no sweet-talking con artist could get them out of it. Not even the notorious Howie.

The cheery sign "Welcome to Winter Hill" belies the history of this section of Somerville. A few blocks from this spot, Buddy McLean, considered the first boss of the Winter Hill Gang, was shot in 1965 while leaving a bar on Broadway. *Photo by Stephanie Schorow.*

Winter also received ten years of jail time for forcing Somerville businessmen to remove pinball machines from their establishments and replace them with machines he owned or controlled. By the time he was paroled, James "Whitey" Bulger and his henchman, Stephen "The Rifleman" Flemmi, had seized control of his crime kingdom. Yet in classic mobster fashion, Winter refused to snitch on the two mob soldiers who had taken over his realm.

After his release from jail in 2002, Winter worked as a property manager and left the mobster life behind. In the 2000s, he sat down with Bobby Martini, the son of a friend, for a series of interviews that appeared in Martini's book about the Irish mob wars, *Citizen Somerville: Growing Up with the Winter Hill Gang.*

## Ilario Maria Antonio Zannino

*Nickname: "Larry"*
*Alias: Larry Baione*
*Born: June 15, 1920, Boston*
*Died: February 27, 1996, Springfield, Missouri*
*Association: Patriarca family*

One of the most prolific bookmakers and loan sharks in New England, Ilario Zannino rose to become a top lieutenant in the Patriarca family. Hard drinking, tough talking and brutal, he was second in command under Gennaro Angiulo, Boston's ruthless mob underboss. Standing five feet, seven inches and weighing 160 pounds, Zannino didn't look like much of a mob heavyweight to outsiders, yet he had a vicious side that would serve him well.

Born in Roxbury, Massachusetts, on June 15, 1920, the son of Joseph Zannino and Isabella LaGrada, he worked as an assistant in his father's shoemaking shop as a youngster. Later, after his family moved to Franklin, Massachusetts, where his mother ran a chicken and pig farm, the young Zannino would gather garbage in the South End to feed the pigs. He also held jobs as a waiter, boxer, nightclub operator and restaurant manager, later moving into racketeering, running Las Vegas nights, loan-sharking and bookmaking. By the 1980s, he had earned enough money to live in a brick mansion on the waterfront in Swampscott, just fifteen miles north of Boston.

# The Men in the Mob

As a teenager at Franklin High School, from which he graduated in 1938, Zannino dreamed of going to medical school. Instead, he became a killer and mob enforcer whose vicious reputation as a hit man made him among the most lethal of mob assassins. Known as "Larry Baione" among his mobster pals, he was nicknamed "Zip" as a youngster, an ironic twist given that a corrupt FBI agent with that same nickname, John "Zip" Connolly, would eventually bring him down.

It is unclear how Zannino got entangled with La Cosa Nostra, but even as a teenager, it seemed he was always looking for trouble. A member of a youth gang called Let's Go, he would roam the streets of the South End hanging off an automobile running board, clutching a revolver, according to *Boston Herald* columnist Howie Carr. Still, he was apparently generous with close friends and family, often giving $500 or $1,000 to friends or relatives who found themselves short on cash. When he attended the 1954 wedding of another former Let's Go gang member, a man who would later go on to become a school principal, he pressed a $100 bill—a fortune at the time—into the groom's hand and curtly said, "Get a necktie, kid."

Convicted in the 1965 murder of a waiter he stabbed to death at a South End restaurant, reportedly because the service was too slow, Zannino also had a conviction for a jewelry heist and so spent much of the 1970s behind bars. He had a reputation for shaking down other mobsters, including Gennaro Angiulo. When Angiulo went to mob boss Raymond Patriarca Sr. with $50,000 in hand and a promise to pay $100,000 annually in tribute, things really turned around. Angiulo's brazen act won over Patriarca, who soon made Zannino an enforcer for the Boston mob boss. It was a relationship that would last the rest of their lives.

Yet Zannino's status in the New England mob didn't get much notice by federal authorities until 1981, when the FBI, with the help of Irish American mobster James "Whitey" Bulger and his pal Stephen "The Rifleman" Flemmi, bugged Angiulo's Prince Street office in Boston's North End. Here, Zannino was often heard by FBI agents discussing mob hits with Angiulo.

"We gotta kill this guy, you know," Zannino is heard on tape saying. The reference was to Angelo Patrizzi, a thirty-eight-year-old ex-con who vowed vengeance against mob leaders for the death of his half brother, killed after he was found skimming money from loan shark receipts. Nicknamed "Hole in the Head" because of the .32-caliber bullet fragments in his skull from a prior shooting episode, Patrizzi had an eighth-grade education, a loud mouth and a grudge that was making the mobsters nervous. Zannino left that meeting with a chilling promise. "I know what to do," he told Angiulo.

Patrizzi's body was later found in the trunk of a stolen car behind the parking lot of a motel in Lynn, Massachusetts. His legs had been hogtied to his neck, and he was stuffed inside a sleeping bag, where he had slowly strangled himself to death.

It wasn't the only murder the feds would seek to pin on Zannino. For years, investigators had been trying to find the killer of mob informant Joseph "The Animal" Barboza, who was shot to death in San Francisco in 1976. In conversations with Angiulo, Zannino identified the hit man as mob capo Joseph "J.R." Russo, who was later considered for the Boston underboss job following Angiulo's arrest on racketeering charges. "We clipped Barboza," Zannino would brag, calling Russo "a genius with a carbine."

Zannino also was suspected of orchestrating a January 30, 1968 car bombing that seriously injured Barboza's attorney, John E. Fitzgerald. The blast ripped off one of Fitzgerald's legs. On tape, Zannino is heard apologizing for not killing Fitzgerald, blaming it on the lawyer's habit of leaving the driver's side door open when starting a car.

In 1987, as federal investigators were wrapping up the trials of several mobsters based on those audiotapes, Zannino was facing a trial of his own. Convicted on racketeering charges for running an illegal gambling operation and extortion, he received a thirty-year prison sentence. While being taken out of the courtroom, a reporter asked what he thought of the verdict. "I hope they all die in their beds," he said, referring to the jury, the *Boston Globe* would report the next day.

It was a typical Zannino outburst but one that would add additional time to his thirty-year sentence. Not that it really mattered. On February 27, 1996, nine years into his incarceration, the tough-talking mobster with the quick trigger finger died of natural causes in a prison hospital in Springfield, Missouri.

## Chapter 3
# HANGOUTS AND HIDEOUTS

### ANGIULO FAMILY HOME

*95 Prince Street, Boston*

The red brick tenement at the corner of Prince and Thatcher Streets looks like all the others in the thickly settled North End section of Boston. Yet its appearance belies its mob history as the birthplace and childhood home of future mob underboss Gennaro Angiulo and his siblings.

Prince Street in Boston's North End marks the territory where the Angiulo brothers once ruled. *Photo by Stephanie Schorow.*

The corner of Prince and Thatcher Streets in the North End was the Angiulo brothers' turf in the 1960s. Gennaro Angiulo lived in one of the apartments on the right. *Photo by Beverly Ford.*

# ANGIULO'S OFFICE

*98 Prince Street, Boston*

Located across the street and just steps from his boyhood home was Gennaro Angiulo's office. Equipped with a full-sized stove for cooking and a television for watching his favorite show, *The Wild, Wild World of Animals*, the 98 Prince Street office provided a private meeting spot to conduct mob business. In 1980, the FBI tuned in to those meetings by planting listening devices inside that office, setting the stage for indictments that would decimate Boston's Italian mob.

Donato Angiulo's office was once located to the rear of this restaurant in the North End. *Photo by Beverly Ford.*

## CAFÉ POMPEII

*280 Hanover Street, Boston*

This North End restaurant, well known for its fine Italian food, is a popular gathering spot for many Bostonians. Yet its red canopied front on busy Hanover Street masks a secret. The back of the restaurant once served as an office for Donato "Danny" Angiulo, a capo in the Patriarca crime family.

## CASTLE ISLAND

*William J. Day Boulevard, South Boston*

The site of one of New England's oldest military forts, Castle Island lives up to its name—it was really once an island, but due to extensive landfill, it is now part of the mainland and a favorite spot for South Boston residents. It has also been a hangout for South Boston's mobsters; James "Whitey" Bulger strolled here often with his lieutenants, away from bugs but often

The seaside setting of Castle Island on Boston Harbor now welcomes runners, fishermen, families and dog walkers. Once, this was a favorite spot for Whitey Bulger; he would walk the shore and talk business with his associates, sometimes under surveillance by authorities. *Photo by Stephanie Schorow.*

under surveillance. South Boston youth gangs often fought turf wars near the Pleasure Bay beach that stretches along William J. Day Boulevard. Kevin Weeks, in his memoir, speaks of dumping the belongings of murder victim Bucky Barrett off a pier here in 1983.

## THE FORMER CHANDLER'S RESTAURANT

*335 Columbus Avenue, South End*

With great Creole dishes served by chef Willard M. Chandler, Chandler's was a restaurant hangout for the criminal elite and likes of James and Johnny Martorano and Howie Winter. A key meeting was held here in the 1970s among representatives of the Winter Hill Gang, the Mullen Gang and the Killeen Gang in an effort to work out a truce. Chef Chandler's efforts to open another restaurant were unfortunately stymied by his association with Winter and James Martorano, who were part owners of the restaurant, but he went on to a storied career cooking at Tim's Tavern, Lulu White's Jazz Club and Chandler's Commonwealth Grill. He died in 1999 at age seventy-nine.

## CHARLES STREET JAIL/LIBERTY HOTEL

*215 Charles Street, Boston*

From 1851 to 1990, the Suffolk County Jail, aka the Charles Street Jail, was the home away from home from many Boston crooks. The jail, located at the foot of Beacon Hill in the shadow of Massachusetts General Hospital, was deliberately built in the center of town as both a warning and a tribute to the idea that prison could change a man. Many of the Brink's robbers cooled their heels here awaiting trial, and in 1954, psychotic hit man Elmer "Trigger" Burke staged a spectacular escape. Other inmates included Gennaro Angiulo, who complained about the accommodations. In 1990, the jail was closed, and in 2007, the Liberty Hotel was opened in the vastly remodeled facility. The luxury hotel, to its credit, does more than nod to its past with a décor that feature bars, a restaurant named Clink and a bar named Alibi. There are also several displays about the jail's history and its role in Boston's law enforcement.

The dramatic interior, which has retained the ninety-foot central rotunda and cupola built in 1851, gives only a faint hint of what it was like to do time here in the past.

## THE SITE OF THE COCOANUT GROVE NIGHTCLUB

*17 Piedmont Street, near corner of Church and Shawmut Streets*

From 1927 until 1942, the Cocoanut Grove nightclub was the place for the high life to meet low life. Gangsters mingled with the political elite, sailors hung out with soldiers and those out for a night on the town dined alongside wedding and anniversary parties. That all changed on the night of November 28, 1942, when fire roared through the nightclub, killing nearly five hundred people and injuring hundreds more. The speed of the fire amazed many, and some looked to the club's shady history for clues.

The Cocoanut Grove was founded in 1927 by bandleader Jacques Renard and entertainer Mickey Alpert, with help from a business investor who turned out to be a swindler. Renard's daughter later told author Stephanie Schorow that her father was threatened by mobsters in connection with ownership of the club, and he eventually left Boston. In 1931, the club passed into the hands of Charles "King" Solomon, a racketeer and bootlegger (see "Charles 'King' Solomon," page 76). Solomon ran the club as his personal showcase until 1933, when he was gunned down at the Cotton Club, another nightspot in the South End, and his lawyer, Barnet "Barney" Welansky, took over the Cocoanut Grove. Welansky worked for a prestigious law firm, but his brother James was known both as a hotel operator and a player on the shady side.

In 1937, James Welansky was managing the Metropolitan Hotel when, in the wee hours of December 17, David J. "Beano" Breen, a known racketeer, gambler and former speakeasy operator, was gunned down in the hotel lobby. Welansky later told police he was standing next to Breen when four shots rang out. The hotel owner didn't see the slayer, know that Breen had been hit or report anything to the police. Instead, he left promptly on a "long-planned trip" to Miami for two months. In May, Welansky returned and insisted the bullets might have been meant for him. Police responded by arresting him for Breen's murder. In July 1938, a grand jury declined to indict him. Welansky returned to the Cocoanut Grove, where he, in his own words, "looked out for my brother's interests."

Brother Barney Welansky focused on more legitimate opportunities. He expanded the Cocoanut Grove and turned it into a profitable enterprise. He also hired unlicensed electrical workers, bragging of his connections to Boston mayor Maurice Tobin, and hid a huge cache of liquor on the premises to avoid paying taxes. In a strange coincidence, he employed as a bookkeeper Rose Gnecco Ponzi, the wife of famed swindler Charles Ponzi, the dubious promoter of pyramid schemes.

On the evening of November 28, 1942, Barney was home sick and James was at the club, hobnobbing with Suffolk County district attorney Garrett Byrne and Boston night police captain James Buccigross, who was supposed to be making his rounds. An upset victory that day of Boston College's football team by Holy Cross had led BC officials to cancel plans to celebrate at the club that night, but the joint was packed with other patrons.

The cause of the fire is a mystery that will not rest. For some, the cause is obvious: about 10:00 p.m., a busboy in a downstairs bar lit a match while replacing a light bulb in a fake coconut tree. The tree caught fire, and the blaze spread with ferocious speed through the entire club. The popular spot was packed, and fleeing patrons found exits locked or blocked and the revolving door of the main entrance jammed from the crush. By the time the fire was out, about 490 people were dead or dying. James Welansky and those at his table managed to escape.

Some have speculated that the fire was set by enemies of the Welanskys, but no hard evidence of this has emerged. Others looked back into the past, wondering if the ghosts of the King Solomon era had some impact. Others have blamed the flammable furnishings and a mysterious gas released from a refrigerator that created the original fireball. What is clear is that someone did not want the truth known. Death threats were made against fire investigators, including State Police detective Philip Deady, whose children attended school under armed guard; attorney Frank Shapiro, who represented victims of the fire; and *Record American* reporter Austen Lake, who wrote multiple stories about the club. The busboy was absolved of culpability (although he would spend the rest of his life under a cloud), and the fire was eventually deemed to be "of unknown origin" by fire officials. In the only conviction involving the fire, Barney Welansky was sentenced to twelve to fifteen years for manslaughter. He was pardoned by Governor Tobin and died a few months later.

Today, the site of the Cocoanut Grove is a parking lot. A plaque made by one of the survivors is set in the sidewalk on Piedmont Street, marking the approximate location of the revolving doors. Often, on the fire's anniversary, flowers are mutely left at the site by those who do not wish to forget.

## THE HOME OF STEPHEN FLEMMI'S PARENTS

*832 East Third Street, South Boston*

When Stephen Flemmi's mother was mugged in her Mattapan neighborhood in 1979 and a photo showing her dazed and bloody sitting on a curb showed up in the local papers, the mobster turned to his pal James "Whitey" Bulger for help. Flemmi wanted to move his parents to a safer Boston neighborhood, and Bulger knew just the place. The home next to his brother, Massachusetts Senate president William "Billy" Bulger, was up for sale. It was the perfect place for Flemmi's aging parents. It also became a convenient meeting spot for the two men and their FBI contacts. Today, the home's all-American look, with its white picket fence and star-spangled flag, gives no hint of what happened behind its closed doors.

Stephen Flemmi bought this house on East Third Street for his mother after she was mugged near her Mattapan home. Surrounded by a white picket fence and flying an American flag, the house sits next door to the home of James "Whitey" Bulger's brother, former Massachusetts Senate president William Bulger. It was here where Bulger strangled Flemmi's girlfriend, Debra Davis, because she allegedly "knew too much." Her body was later moved down the street to a second house on East Third Street, where her remains were buried in the basement. Her remains were moved again to a spot near the Neponset River in Quincy after the second home was put up for sale. *Photo by Beverly Ford.*

# FRANCESCO'S RESTAURANT

*90 North Washington Street, Boston*

A favorite eating and meeting spot for underworld figures, Francesco's was popular with FBI agents too—at least on the night of September 19, 1983. As Gennaro Angiulo sat eating with two of his brothers, federal agents walked into the restaurant and arrested all three on racketeering charges. Handcuffed, Angiulo walked out muttering that he would be "back before the pork chops are cold." The restaurant, which has changed hands several times since that night, is now a trendy, upscale eatery that serves pizza, pasta and other Italian specialties.

The restaurant on North Washington Street in the North End where the Angiulos were arrested in 1983 is now a modern, upscale eatery serving pizza, pasta and other specialties. *Photo by Beverly Ford.*

# JAY'S LOUNGE

*253 Tremont Street, Boston*

Jay's Lounge, a Tremont Street restaurant and bar, became a hangout for mobster and owner Gennaro Angiulo's pals and business associates. The bar and a basement office were also the subject of wiretap surveillance by investigators probing Angiulo's ties to gambling and loan-sharking. Situated in Boston's seedy Combat Zone, once a neighborhood of strip joints, gay bars and prostitutes, it has since been renamed and remodeled into an upscale eatery now located in the center of Boston's thriving Theater District.

## JOHN JOSEPH MULLEN SQUARE

*O Street and East Second Street, South Boston*

The Irish gang that emerged in South Boston in the 1940s was supposedly named for the square that honored veteran John Joseph Mullen at the intersection of O Street and East Second Street in South Boston. The Mullen Gang once fought the Killeen Gang for dominance in Boston, and its members eventually merged with the Winter Hill Gang. The square sits in a tight-knit neighborhood of multi-family homes, just a few blocks from Pleasure Bay.

## KNIGHTS OF COLUMBUS HALL

*41 North Margin Street, Boston*

Housed in an imposing red brick building on North Margin Street just around the corner from the Angiulo family home in Boston's North End, the Knights of Columbus Hall was a gathering spot for many Italian men, among them Donato Angiulo. The fraternal organization behind those brick walls and iron fences dates back to the sixteenth century.

The Knights of Columbus Hall in the North End where Donato Angiulo often hung out. The building is just around the corner from his childhood home on Prince Street. *Photo by Beverly Ford.*

## LANCASTER STREET GARAGE

*Lancaster Street, near Merrimack Street*

An aging flophouse at 119 Merrimack Street in Boston provided state police investigators with the perfect undercover location to spy on the headquarters of the Winter Hill Gang, located in the Lancaster Street Garage. From a room overlooking the garage on Lancaster Street in Boston's North End, authorities watched the comings and goings of some of the region's biggest mob names, snapping photos as evidence. But when an electronic listening device was installed in the garage, it picked up nothing incriminating. It would be years before investigators found out why. An FBI agent, eager to protect his informants, had tipped them off to the investigation.

As state police investigators watched from a window across the street, mobsters conducted business around this garage on Lancaster Street. The garage, just steps from the Boston Garden, home to the city's beloved Celtics and Bruins, became the headquarters for Whitey Bulger and his cronies. *Photo by Beverly Ford.*

## MARSHALL MOTORS

*12–14 Marshall Street, Somerville*

The garage on a side street off Broadway in Somerville's Winter Hill neighborhood was once the epicenter for criminal planning in the area. The auto repair shop was owned by Howie Winter, the onetime head of the Winter Hill Gang, and frequented by his crew, including James "Whitey"

*Above*: The site of a Winter Hill Gang–run business: Marshall Motors in Somerville on Marshall Street, now, ironically, a church. *Photo by Stephanie Schorow.*

*Left*: This Winter Hill Bakery was once the site of Pal Joey, a bar and hangout for the Winter Hill Gang. *Photo by Stephanie Schorow.*

Bulger, Stephen "The Rifleman" Flemmi, Johnny Martorano and others. Winter lived on Marshall Street nearby. Today, the former garage is a church. Just around the corner is another Winter Hill Gang hangout, a bar once called 318 Lounge and then Pal Joey's. It is now a bakery.

## Neponset River Bridge

*Quincy, Massachusetts*

The brush and wetlands at the banks of the Neponset River, near the bridge of I-93, was a convenient location for the disposal of murder victims for Boston's pitiless killers. Tommy King, who was gunned down by hit man Johnny Martorano at the behest of Whitey Bulger, was buried here. Martorano would later testify in 2002 that when he and Bulger would drive over the bridge into Quincy, Whitey would say, "Tip your hat to Tommy."

## South Boston Liquor Mart

*295 Old Colony Avenue, Boston*

The liquor store at the rotary on Old Colony Avenue in South Boston remains a landmark even though it has changed hands several times since

In 1984, Whitey Bulger took over what was then called Stippo's Liquor Mart at 295 Old Colony. The store was owned by a young South Boston couple when Bulger decided he wanted it and made an offer they couldn't refuse. The newly named South Boston Liquor Mart was at the heart of Whitey's enterprises in South Boston. *Photo by Stephanie Schorow.*

St. Monica's Church in South Boston, where the Bulger brothers and John Connolly attended Mass as children. The church is just steps from the Old Colony projects where the Bulgers grew up and from the Rotary Liquor Store, owned by Whitey Bulger. *Photo by Beverly Ford.*

Whitey Bulger and his associates allegedly forced owners Stephen and Julie Rakes to sell the store, named Stippo's Liquor Mart, to the mobster in 1984. Years later, it would be known as the place where a Bulger associate bought a winning $14 million lottery ticket that he shared with Bulger and the mobster's sidekick, Kevin Weeks. The store, located less than a block from St. Monica's Church, where Bulger and his future FBI handler John Connolly worshiped as children, is still well known in Southie for its past mob affiliations.

## TRIPLE O's BAR

*28 West Broadway, South Boston*

Once a favorite hangout of James "Whitey" Bulger and his Winter Hill friends, Triple O's was a popular watering hole for thirsty Southie residents looking for a cool brew or a quick bite to eat. It was here that Bulger held court over his minions, collecting unpaid debts, working the numbers racket and sometimes even plotting a murder or two. Here, Brian Halloran

The location of the former Triple O's bar at 28 West Broadway in South Boston was once a hangout for Whitey Bulger and his crew. *Photo by Stephanie Schorow.*

escorted a bookie named Louis Latif to a meeting with Bulger, only to see the mobster and another pal haul Latif's plastic-wrapped body out a back door just minutes later. It was also at this Southie gathering spot where Kevin Weeks found a job as a bouncer—and a career in the Irish mob. Today, rechristened the Owl Station Bar and Bistro, Bulger's once notorious hangout caters to an upscale crowd of gentrified South Boston residents.

## Chapter 4
# HITS AND HEISTS

### The Bennett Brothers

*Edward A. Bennett*
*Disappeared January 1967*
*Walter Bennett*
*Disappeared April 1967*
*William F. "Billy" Bennett*
*Body Dumped on Harvard Street, Dorchester, December 23, 1967*

Edward A. "Wimpy" Bennett was a prime player in Boston's underworld in the late 1950s to mid-1960s, and his murder was the first of three that would decimate his family. In 1967, according to the *Boston Globe*, Bennett was described by police as "possibly the most powerful influence in Boston crime outside the Cosa Nostra." He got the nickname "Wimpy" because he relished hamburgers like Popeye's sidekick. But he was also known as "The Fox."

Bennett played a role in the infamous 1950 Brink's robbery (see "The Brink's Heist," page 113), although his exact part has never been made clear. After serving a one-year term in the House of Corrections on Deer Island from 1956 to 1957 for receiving stolen money from the Brink's robbery, Bennett went on to be the banker for loan shark operations; his crew included the two Flemmi brothers, Stephen and Vincent. "After Jerry Angiulo, Wimpy the Fox probably had more money than anybody else in

Boston—he had a piece of everything in Roxbury," as John Martorano told Howie Car in *Hitman: The Untold Story of Johnny Martorano.* In January 1967, the forty-seven-year-old vanished; his disappearance was not reported to authorities until early March, when he failed to show up for the funeral of his wife, Jennie, on March 9. Francis "Cadillac Frank" Salemme and Stephen Flemmi later admitted to handling the hit and said they buried the body at a gun range in Hopkington. (Vincent Teresa contends in his book *My Life in the Mafia* that Flemmi and Salemme dumped Wimpy's body in lye in a construction project that's now part of Interstate 93.) His was the first in three slaying involving the Bennett brothers.

Walter Bennett, fifty-five, who operated a café on Dudley Street in Roxbury, was understandably angry when his younger brother disappeared, and he vowed to find the killers. Salemme and Flemmi again took action. Bennett disappeared on April 3; his car was found the next day at Logan airport, but his body was never found.

William F. "Billy" Bennett, fifty-six, also vowed to do something about the fate of his two brothers. On December 23, his body was thrown from a car on Harvard Street in Dorchester in front of the Audubon School; he had been shot four times in the chest. A convict turned informant, Robert Daddieco, later fingered himself and five others for the Billy Bennett slaying: Salemme, Flemmi, Richard Grasso, Peter Poulos and Hugh J. "Sonny" Shields. Grasso, a friend of Billy who picked him up the night he was shot, apparently couldn't stop talking about the hit and was also marked for death. Six days later, the body of this thirty-four-year-old South Boston man, with two bullets to the head, was found in the trunk of his 1967 Buick Wildcat sedan left in Brookline. Poulos was later killed by Flemmi.

In 2001 and again in 2003, Flemmi and Salemme led authorities to the Hopkinton Sportsmen's Association on Lumber Street, where they said the Bennetts had been buried. After several weeks of digging, however, no bodies were found.

The children of Edward and Walter Bennett later filed multimillion-dollar lawsuits against the U.S. government and the late H. Paul Rico, contending that that he and the FBI allowed Flemmi to murder their fathers because at the time he was an FBI informant.

## BLACKFRIARS MASSACRE

*Blackfriars Pub*
*105 Summer Street, Downtown Crossing*

The name alone can send shivers down the spine of longtime Bostonians: Blackfriars. On June 28, 1978, a janitor reported for work at 4:00 a.m. and found five bodies in an office of the bar/disco, just blocks from the heart of Boston's retail district. All had been shot in the head, probably around 2:00 a.m., and blood covered the walls and floors. Among the dead was the owner of the restaurant, Vincent Solmonte, age thirty-five, and John A. "Jack" Kelly, thirty-four, a well-known investigative TV and radio reporter intimately familiar with Boston's murky underworld. Also slain were Peter Meroth, thirty-one, of Jamaica Plain; Freddy R. Delavega, thirty-four, of Somerville; and Charles G. Magarian, twenty-six, of North Andover. They had been in the midst of a backgammon game when they were murdered.

The motive for the slaying seemed murky, and many feared it signaled a return to the violent gangland warfare of the 1960s. Kelly, who had done exposés on alleged liquor license payoffs, was known to be close to underworld figures. Kelly "liked nothing better than to sit at a bar with people like Howie Winter and Jimmy Martorano and Frankie Salemme and all the rest as if he were one of them," *Boston Globe* reporters Richard Connelly and Douglas S. Crocket wrote. Friends of Kelly lamented the demise of a tenacious, aggressive reporter, wondering if he had gotten in over his head. "He was attracted to mobsters like a moth to a candle," journalist Maurice Lewis told the *Phoenix*, Boston's alternative newspaper, in a story published on July 4, 1978. "He started to cultivate mob contacts as a way of getting into investigative reporting back before it became fashionable. And he loved that movie image. I don't think he ever thought of it as anything other than a movie. But it was very real, and he just kept getting in deeper and deeper." Kelly's underworld contacts eventually ran afoul of his TV bosses, and he was fired. At the time of the massacre, he was working as the night manager of Blackfriars, which was known as a swinging disco as well as a hangout for underworld types.

But the massacre may have had nothing to do with Kelly: Solmonte, who also owned another restaurant, was an alleged cocaine dealer. Police concluded that the massacre was the result of a drug deal gone wrong; cocaine, marijuana and stacks of cash were found at the scene. Two men—

This block of downtown Boston at the intersection of Summer and Bedford Streets once housed the Blackfriars Pub, scene of an infamous gangland massacre in June 1978. Five men were shot to death while playing backgammon in the basement of this pub/disco in what was a heist of $36,500 in cash and three pounds of cocaine. The dead included Jack Kelly, a TV investigative reporter and part owner of the pub. No one was ever convicted of the crime. *Photo by Stephanie Schorow.*

Robert J. Italiano, thirty-six, of Everett, and William N. Ierardi, thirty-three, of East Boston—were arrested and charged with the murders but were found not guilty after a twenty-seven-day trial. No one was ever convicted of the crime.

Blackfriars is long gone, and the remodeled block shows no trace of the former nightspot.

## ARTHUR BRATSOS AND THOMAS J. DEPRISCO

*Nite Lite Café, Commercial Street, Boston*

An act of loyalty cost Arthur "Tash" Bratsos and Thomas J. DePrisco their lives. The two men, pals to Joseph "The Animal" Barboza, were trying to raise money to meet Barboza's $100,000 bail when they stopped at an underworld hangout, the Nite Lite Café on Commercial Street, in the fall of 1966. The men had already raised $59,000 to bail Barboza, who was being held on a weapons charge, when they walked into the nightspot just a half block from Hanover Street in the North End looking for donors. Unfortunately, Bratsos and DePrisco tried to shake down the wrong crowd. Their bullet-riddled bodies were found on November 1, 1966, inside the trunk of Bratsos's black Cadillac in South Boston. The killers parked the car in Boston's primarily Irish Southie neighborhood to divert police suspicion to Irish gangsters and away from the Italian mob, which actually committed the murders. In the end, the killers were never found. Neither was the $59,000 the victims had raised to free Barboza.

## THE BRINK'S HEIST

*North Terminal Garage*
*Corner of Prince and Commercial Street, North End*

The sensational 1950 heist of $1.2 million in cash from the Brink's armored car headquarters in Boston made international headlines not just because it was the largest armed robbery in U.S. history to date. More importantly

The North Terminal Garage in the North End on Prince Street, once the headquarters of Brink's armored car service in Boston and the scene of a massive heist in 1950. *Photo by Stephanie Schorow.*

to Bostonians, who took a perverse pride in the caper, the robbery was a bloodless crime. The Brink's guards were roughed up but not injured. The seven masked bandits flashed guns but did not fire a shot. The getaway was clean, and despite a statewide manhunt, no suspects were immediately targeted. The crime was so perfect that reporters like Joseph F. Dinneen of the *Boston Globe* speculated that no Hub gangsters were smart enough to pull off what was dubbed "the crime of the century."

But from the cool perspective of history, the seemingly flawless crime left a trail of blood and ruined lives and a body count that piled up as the years went on. While some of the thieves turned out to be petty Boston criminals, a few were well connected with organized crime in New York and Rhode Island and did not hesitate to turn lethal when they thought their ill-gotten gains were at risk. By the time of the trial in the fall of 1956, the sheen was off the bright luster of the robbery, and the convicted culprits were sentenced to hard time for their part in the crime.

The robbery took place about 7:00 p.m. on a cold January 17, when seven men in grotesque masks and dressed alike in pea coats and chauffeur's hats surprised Brink's guards just as they were preparing to lock the day's money transfers in a secure vault in the company's office on the second floor of the North Terminal Garage, a three-level building bounded by Prince Street, Commercial Street, Hull Street and Snowhill Avenue. In less than twenty minutes, the guards were bound up, and the bandits had moved a huge amount of cash and securities into a getaway car parked at the Prince Street entrance. The only evidence left at the scene were the rope and tape used to tie up the guards and one chauffeur's hat. The getaway car was later found dismantled in a Stoughton dump.

Police and FBI soon targeted a group of known criminals who could have pulled off the job, including Anthony Pino, his brother-in-law Vincent James Costa, Thomas Francis "Sandy" Richardson and Joseph James "Specky" O'Keefe. Fingers were also pointed at Joe McGinnis, a bar owner and money launderer, who was not above watering down his drinks and making his own liquor to avoid taxes. But despite a long investigation by FBI and Boston police and a grand jury convened in 1954, mouths stayed shut, and no charges would stick. Meanwhile, O'Keefe and fellow thief Stanley "Gus" Gusciora were arrested for robbery in Pennsylvania and jailed. On his release, O'Keefe demanded his share of the Brink's loot, which he had given to a fellow robber for safekeeping (and who had gambled it away). O'Keefe became so persistent that New York hit man Elmer "Trigger" Burke was brought in, probably by Pino, to silence him (see "Elmer Francis Burke,"

The robbers of the Brink's headquarters in January 1950 pulled off what appeared to be the perfect crime—the biggest armed robbery thus far in American history. Despite their meticulous planning, one of the robbers dropped his hat at the scene, a chauffeur's cap. It remains in the possession of the FBI in Washington, D.C. *Photo by Stephanie Schorow.*

page 39). Just a week before the state statute of limitations on the crime would run out, O'Keefe was finally persuaded to rat out the gang.

On January 11, 1956, arrest warrants were issued for Pino, Costa, Gusciora, McGinnis, Richardson, Vincent Geagan, Henry Baker, James Ignatius "Jimma" Faherty and bookie Adolph "Jazz" Maffie. The getaway car driver, Barney Banfield, had died, and Gus, the youngest of the bunch, would die before the trial began. Richardson and Faherty eluded a dragnet and achieved the dubious honoring of making the FBI's most wanted list.

It turned out that the masterminds of the crime of the century were a motley crew, as well as a little United Nations of criminals. Pino and Costa represented the Italian side and O'Keefe and McGinnis the Irish side. Henry Baker, a skilled safecracker whom Pino had met in the slammer, was Jewish. This set the tone for a number of barroom debates: was the Brink's job an Irish crime or an Italian crime? What is also clear is that death is an equal opportunity employer. In what Boston reporters labeled the "Brink's Jinx," a bloody swath cut through the hitherto violence-free crime. The victims included:

CARLTON M. O'BRIEN: The Rhode Island restaurant owner and friend of McGinnis was shot down in his front yard in May 1952 days after he was named as a mastermind of the robbery. The murder was never solved, but it was likely at the command of boss Raymond Patriarca Sr., who saw O'Brien as a threat to his power in Rhode Island.

JOHN HENRY "JOHNNY" CARLSON: The South End bookie was a good pal of O'Keefe and helped him after O'Keefe was wounded by Trigger Burke in June 1954. A month later, Carlson disappeared; his body was never found. He had been seen talking to Suffolk County district attorney Garrett H. Byrne.

GEORGE D. O'BRIEN: O'Brien, a friend to Pino, was a suspect in the Brink's robbery. But O'Brien had his own fish to fry. In March 1952, $681,700 was brazenly stolen from a Brink's armored car in Danvers when the driver left to get a cup of coffee. After O'Brien bought a new house and car, police swooped in and found stashes of cash through his home. He was charged with the Danvers job. Yet thanks to his resourceful lawyer, Paul Smith (who would also represent some of the Brink's robbers in their trial), O'Brien was found not guilty of the spectacular theft. His relief was short-lived; on June 17, 1954, O'Brien was found dying inside his car in Franklin Park, shot once in the head with a .38-caliber revolver discovered in his lap. Police called it suicide, which no one believed, particularly because his death came at the time hit man Trigger Burke was in Boston.

WILLIAM CAMERON: A South Boston longshoreman and Dorchester resident, Cameron may have tipped off authorities to the location of Brink's suspects Thomas "Sandy" Richardson and James I. Faherty, who were picked up on May 16, 1956, four months after they were indicted for the Brink's job. On June 10, 1956, Cameron's body was found slumped at the wheel of his car behind the Fargo Building on Summer Street, with two .38-caliber bullets through his head. He was forty-nine years old. Cameron was also heavily involved with other illegal operations that could have led to his untimely demise.

Just before the Brink's trial was to start, a Boston man with underworld ties attempted to use a musty ten-dollar bill in a Baltimore amusement park. A suspicious arcade operator alerted police, who found that the serial numbers on the bills matched those known in the Brink's robbery. Quickly, the police grabbed the man, and he led them to a construction company office on Tremont Street in the South End, where John F. "Fats" Buccelli and Edward "Wimpy" Bennett ran a contracting business. Behind a false wall, authorities found a stash of about $57,000 in mildewed bills—most of it from the Brink's job. This is the only cash from the $1.2 million haul ever found. The location or fate of the rest remains a mystery.

After a two-month trial, in October 1956, the eight Brink's defendants were found guilty and given long jail terms. Baker and McGinnis died in prison; the others were paroled over the years, the last being Pino in 1971. For his cooperation, O'Keefe was released in the 1960s and resettled in California. Both Buccelli and Bennett received short jail sentences for receiving stolen money and went on to suffer grisly fates (see "The Bennett Brothers," page 109, and "John F. 'Fats' Buccelli," page 117). Jazz Maffie and Sandy Richardson lived long enough to be treated as folk heroes when the movie *The Brink's Job* was released. Costa, alas, could not stay out of trouble and was jailed twice more for counterfeiting and drug dealing.

The Brink's robbery represented a kind of transition in Boston's underworld from an era in which violence was avoided when possible to an even more lethal and cold-blooded code of conduct. By the 1960s, Irish and Italian mobsters were at war with one another—and among themselves—and Boston's gangland landscape was increasingly littered with bodies. In retrospect, the Brink's robbery looks almost quaint.

## John F. "Fats" Buccelli

*Castle Square, Arlington and Chandler Street, South End, Boston*

When John F. "Fats" Buccelli was released on May 19, 1958, after serving eighteen months of a two-year sentence for receiving money stolen in the infamous Brink's case, Suffolk County district attorney Garrett Byrne made a prediction to *Globe* reporter Jerome Sullivan: "This man won't live a day if he is allowed on the street." Turns out, Byrne should have made it a month. Buccelli, a three-hundred-pound wise guy, was well known to the Brink's gang. At some point, he received a cache of money from the heist that should have been destroyed, as the serial numbers could be linked to the robbery. The money, buried for a number of years, was discovered hidden in a picnic cooler behind a false wall in a business Buccelli helped run in the South End with Edward "Wimpy" Bennett. Even while jailed in the House of Corrections on Deer Island for his part in the Brink's caper, Buccelli was indicted by the federal government for participating in a multimillion-dollar narcotics ring. He was said to be the Boston contact for a wharf that was used as a drug drop. He posted bail for the narcotics rap and was out of jail by May 19. On June 19, his body was found, shot twice in the back of the head, in a plush sedan near the corner of Arlington and Chandler Streets in the South End. He was forty-four years old. The murder was never solved.

## EDWARD "TEDDY" DEEGAN

*Alley off Fourth Street, Chelsea, Massachusetts*

The hit on longshoreman and small potatoes hood Edward "Teddy" Deegan would not even qualify as a footnote in Boston mob annals except for one crucial outcome: four men were wrongly imprisoned for decades for his murder, and the case became a cause célèbre and a lesson in the miscarriage of justice. On March 12, 1965, Deegan's body was found shot five times in the back of the head in an alleyway in Chelsea, a working-class town just outside of Boston. The thirty-five-year-old with a long criminal background and who was a suspect in a $40,000 holdup of a local bookie was lured there on the pretext of participating in a burglary. What only became clear years later was that the FBI—in particular H. Paul Rico—had known that a hit on Deegan was being planned due to bugs planted in the offices of Raymond Patriarca Sr. in his Providence headquarters. Vincent "Jimmy the Bear" Flemmi, who was to become an FBI informant, was heard on the bugs complaining about Deegan's behavior at a Revere nightclub; Flemmi told Patriarca he wanted Deegan taken out. Two days later, Deegan was shot. The FBI did nothing to warn Deegan he was a target. Deegan's murder went officially unsolved until 1967, when Joe "The Animal" Barboza was convinced to be a witness against Patriarca and others. Barboza confessed to the Deegan murder but named Joseph Salvati, Peter J. Limone, Louis Greco and Henry Tameleo as accomplices. The FBI did nothing as the four were convicted and sentenced to life in prison. Tameleo, eighty-four, and Greco, seventy-eight, died in prison. Vincent Flemmi died in 1979. In the late 1990s, the complicated relationship among the FBI, the Flemmi brothers and other informants was revealed, leading to the exoneration of Limone and Salvati, both then in their sixties. "It was more important for the FBI to protect its murderous informants than it was to protect the lives of innocent men and their families," Medford lawyer Victor J. Garo, who represented Salvati, later told reporters. While many, including some in the FBI, took the attitude that the convicted foursome were guilty of *something*, convicting them for a crime they did not commit does not meet the standards of American justice.

# DEPOSITORS TRUST BANK HEIST

*55 High Street, Medford, Massachusetts*

Over the Memorial Day weekend in May 1980, a persistent group of thieves broke into a vault at the Depositors Trust Bank on High Street in Medford Square and made off with cash and valuables stashed in more than one thousand safe deposit boxes. The cash alone topped $1.5 million. It turned out that the thieves included Gerald W. Clemente Jr., a Metropolitan Police captain, as well as a Metropolitan Police sergeant and a Medford police lieutenant. Two mobsters were also involved, including master safecracker and drug dealer Arthur "Bucky" Barrett of Quincy. Convicted in 1986, Clemente later wrote a book on the crime, *The Cops Are Robbers*, which inspired a 1990 TV movie.

Unfortunately for Barrett, his associate James "Whitey" Bulger decided that he had been cut out of his fair share of the loot. In 1983, he, Steven Flemmi and Kevin J. Weeks carried out an elaborate plan in which they lured Barrett to a house on East Third Street in South Boston with the promise of selling some "hot" diamonds. According to Weeks's memoir, Barrett walked into the trap. Bulger and Flemmi quizzed Barrett at gunpoint about his drug deals, demanded and got money from him and then shot him in the back of the head. Barrett's body was buried, along with victims Deborah Hussey and John McIntyre, in Dorchester. In January 2000, after Weeks struck a deal with investigators and started talking, the bodies were exhumed. In another tragic footnote, two of Barrett's sons committed suicide by throwing themselves in front of trains—a circumstance that some members of the Barrett family found suspicious.

Today, the Depositors Trust building is occupied by Salvatore's, a fine Italian restaurant. Framed photos and news clippings tell the story of the 1980 crime, and there's a small dining area in the bank's former vault, complete with the polished metal door.

# BRIAN HALLORAN AND MICHAEL DONAHUE

*Anthony's Pier 4 Restaurant, 140 Northern Avenue, South Boston*

Edward Brian Halloran was a low-level hoodlum with a big mouth and a short lifespan. Known as "Balloonhead," he was an associate of James "Whitey" Bulger, and he was at Triple O's bar in 1980 when Louis Latif was killed. Halloran was first asked to do the 1981 hit on Tulsa businessman Roger Wheeler but was later paid off and told to "never mind." But the drug-addicted father of two began to fear he was marked for execution. Desperate to save his own skin, Halloran went to the FBI and offered to snitch on the Winter Hill Gang in exchange for protection. Soon, the cocaine addict was talking about the Wheeler and Latif murders and fingering Bulger as the killer. When FBI agent John Connolly learned Halloran was spilling his guts, he wrote a report that prompted the FBI to cut Halloran loose as an untrustworthy informant. Within weeks, Halloran was dead, cut down in a restaurant parking lot by a burst of bullets. On May 11, 1982, a pal, Michael Donahue, had met up with Halloran for dinner at Anthony's Pier 4 restaurant and innocently offered his friend a ride home. As their car pulled out of the parking lot, two gunmen approached armed with a carbine, a Mac 10 and silencers, and within minutes, both men were dead. With his dying breath, Halloran identified his killer as James Flynn, an associate of the Winter Hill Gang, but the man under that brown Afro wig and mustache was none other than James "Whitey" Bulger. Flynn was later tried and acquitted. It would take nearly eighteen years before another informant, Kevin Weeks, would identify the killer as Bulger. Halloran's and Donahue's families would later file a multimillion-dollar lawsuit against the FBI, alleging that the agency had failed to protect the victims. Their lawsuit was rejected by the U.S. Appeals Court.

## THE IRISH MOB WARS

### 1961–76
#### Boston, Charlestown, Somerville and Beyond

One of the bloodiest gang wars in New England started over a woman and ended with nearly fifty people dead. The first salvo in the altercation was fired on Labor Day 1961, when gang members from Boston's Charlestown neighborhood and Irish gangsters from Winter Hill in nearby Somerville crossed paths at a beach party while celebrating the end of summer.

GEORGE MCLAUGHLIN, a Charlestown crew hoodlum, was drunk when he groped a woman (reputed to be the girlfriend of Winter Hill gangster Alex Rocco, at the time known as ALEX "BOBO" PETRICONE). The incident sparked an attack on McLaughlin that left him bruised, bleeding and nearly

# Hits and Heists

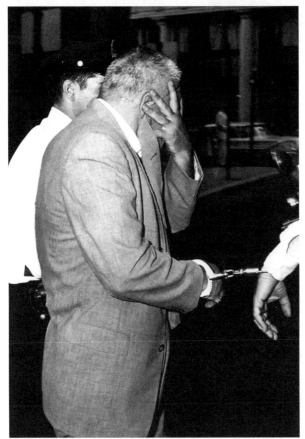

*Above*: The murder scene of Edward "Punchy" McLaughlin is reenacted in chilling detail by teens in the area where Punchy was gunned down. A former boxer and freelance hit man for gangs throughout New England, McLaughlin was shot dead in October 1965 outside a West Roxbury bus station while on the way to his brother's murder trial. *Courtesy of the Boston Public Library.*

*Left*: Edward "Punchy" McLaughlin hides his face in this 1962 photo. *Courtesy of the Boston Public Library, Print Department.*

Edward "Punchy" McLaughlin. *Courtesy of the Boston Public Library, Print Department.*

dead. Believing he had indeed expired, the Winter Hill crew loaded McLaughlin's body into a car and dumped him on the lawn of a hospital.

A furious BERNIE MCLAUGHLIN, head of the Charlestown mob, paid a visit to BUDDY MCLEAN, the Winter Hill Gang leader, and demanded that the two men involved in his brother's beating be killed. When McLean refused, Bernie McLaughlin stormed out of the meeting. Later, McLean found a makeshift bomb strapped under the hood of his car. On Halloween 1961, just one day later, McLean shot Bernie McLaughlin to death in front of about one hundred witnesses in Charlestown's City Square.

About two years later, in 1964, George McLaughlin shot twenty-year-old WILLIAM SHERIDAN to death in Roxbury in the mistaken belief that he had argued with Sheridan earlier at a party. That same year, ex-con FRANK BENJAMIN was murdered and decapitated after a drunken Benjamin bragged about icing the entire Winter Hill Gang. VINCENT "THE BEAR" FLEMMI, overhearing Benjamin's remarks, pulled out his gun and shot the braggart dead and then cut off his head, hoping to leave it on the doorstep of EDWARD "PUNCHY" MCLAUGHLIN, a brother of George and Bernie. Instead, Flemmi stuffed Sheridan's decapitated body in the trunk of a car and buried his head in the woods.

The war escalated. Eight days later, on May 12, the Charlestown gang killed RUSSELL NICHOLSON, an ex-cop now working as Buddy McLean's bodyguard. Three months later, the Winter Hill crew killed two Charlestown associates by luring them to a woman's apartment. Before completing the job, however, McLean held a blowtorch to the men's genitals to get information and then strangled them, dumping their bodies into Boston Harbor.

On September 2 of that same year, Ronald Dermondy burst into a café on Broadway in Winter Hill and shot a man he believed was McLean. In

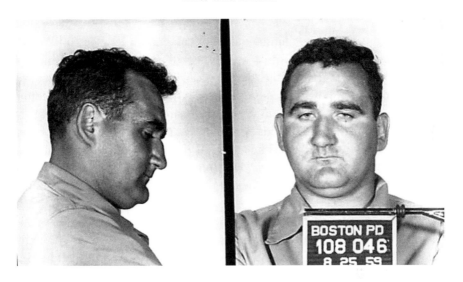

*Above*: Cornelius "Connie" Hughes's mug shot. *Courtesy of the Boston Public Library, Print Department.*

*Below*: The murder scene of Cornelius "Connie" Hughes, who was cut down while driving on an expressway in Revere. *Courtesy of the Boston Public Library, Print Department.*

exchange for the murder, Dermondy had negotiated a deal with George McLaughlin to kill the boyfriend of a woman Dermondy was in love with. But he made one serious mistake. He had killed an innocent man. When McLean found out about the error, he hired JOSEPH "THE ANIMAL" BARBOZA to take down the lovelorn shooter. Dermondy's body was found on September 4 inside his car at a red light in Watertown, Massachusetts.

Throughout 1965, the killings continued. Then, on October 20, Punchy McLaughlin was shot dead while waiting for a bus that would take him to his brother George's trial for the murder of William Sheridan. Barboza, the triggerman, and two of his pals shot Punchy a total of nine times, including twice in the genitals and once in the face. Punchy had already survived two previous attempts on his life, but he couldn't outrun fate. Eleven days later, McLean was shot and killed as he left a bar on Broadway in Somerville by STEPHEN AND CORNELIUS "CONNIE" HUGHES, a pair of McLaughlin loyalists. The murder occurred four years nearly to the day of Bernie McLaughlin's homicide.

With the two gang leaders, McLean and Punchy McLaughlin, now dead and George McLaughlin serving time on death row, many thought the bloody attacks were finally over. Instead, it continued, with the Hughes brothers as the next target.

Sons of a Charlestown shipyard electrician who was jailed for possession of a machine gun, Connie and Steve Hughes amassed records of robbery, assault and intent to murder at a young age. On May 25, 1966, a speeding car pulled up alongside that of Connie Hughes as he was driving home on Route 1 to Malden through Revere. Connie's car was riddled with bullets and smashed

A 1984 FBI mug shot of Whitey Bulger. *FBI file photo.*

into an abutment. Connie, age thirty-six, died at the scene. On September 23, in a similar hit, Stephen Hughes and another man were cut down in a hail of bullets while they were driving along Route 114 in Middleton in the mid-afternoon. Both Steve, age thirty-nine, and the other man were killed.

The hits continued until 1972, when forty-eight-year-old DONALD KILLEEN, head of another Irish crew known as the Killeen Gang, was gunned down in his car outside his Framingham home. He was the third Killeen brother to die in the gangland war.

With Killeen dead, JAMES "WHITEY" BULGER, a Killeen associate, seized control of the gang but soon turned to HOWIE WINTER, now head of the Winter Hill Gang, to help mediate a truce to put an end to all the shootings. In exchange, Bulger brought all the rackets in South Boston under his own control, merging members of the Mullen Gang into it as well, while serving as an underboss to Winter. From 1966 to 1976, the now revitalized Winter Hill Gang killed thirteen men to become the second-largest criminal organization in Massachusetts next to La Cosa Nostra. When the bloodletting finally ended, forty-eight were dead and many were in prison.

## THE JAI ALAI KILLINGS

*Roger M. Wheeler Sr.*
*Tulsa, Oklahoma*
*John B. Callahan*
*Miami, Florida*

Roger M. Wheeler Sr. and John B. Callahan thought they had hit the good time in the late 1970s—until, that is, they crossed the path of James "Whitey" Bulger. The two businessmen met their fates far from New England, but their doom was planned in Boston and was intricately linked to the harsh dictates of Boston's underworld.

Wheeler, a Tulsa, Oklahoma–based businessman, was the multimillionaire owner of World Jai Alai, a company that promoted this fast-paced game that originated in Spain's Basque region as a parimutuel gambling option. (The game is popular among Latin Americans, Brazilians and Spaniards.) As the company's president from 1974 to 1976 and then a consultant, Callahan had arranged the sale of the company in 1978 to Wheeler. With Jai Alai frontons (or playing areas) in Florida and Connecticut, the money was rolling in, and Bulger couldn't help but notice. Wanting a cut of the action, Bulger and fellow mobster Stephen

"The Rifleman" Flemmi arranged to skim an estimated $10,000 weekly from the parking lot operations at the company's Connecticut gaming facility. Having one of his former FBI handlers, H. Paul Rico, look the other way while working as the head of security for World Jai Alai certainly helped.

However, Wheeler, the fifty-five-year-old former chairman of Telex Corp. and the father of five children, was growing suspicious, which threatened to unravel the skimming scheme. With prompting by Callahan, Bulger and Flemmi made sure that would never happen. They issued a contract on his life. On May 27, 1981, hit man Johnny Martorano put a bullet between Wheeler's eyes as he got into his car after a round of golf at Southern Hills Country Club in Tulsa, killing him instantly. Rico provided Martorano with the necessary information for the hit.

Just one year later, the man who was first offered the Wheeler murder contract, Brian Halloran, another Bulger associate and a friend of Callahan, was shot dead after leaving a waterfront restaurant in South Boston with a buddy, who was also killed. Halloran had made the mistake of going to the FBI to tell them about the Wheeler hit.

Callahan, a forty-five-year-old flamboyant Boston businessman with a house in a tony suburb and two kids, was questioned about the business practices of World Jai Alai but was never arrested or indicted. But Bulger feared that Callahan would tell authorities about the skimming scheme, as well as the Wheeler and Halloran murders. On August 3, 1982, Callahan's body was found stuffed in the trunk of his rented Cadillac at Miami International Airport when a parking lot attendant noticed a stench. Authorities had been trying to locate him for questioning. A prosecutor later said FBI agent John Connolly told Bulger and Flemmi that Callahan would likely implicate them in Wheeler's slaying.

Martorano, who confessed to killing both Wheeler and Callahan, served twelve years in prison and is now free after cutting a deal. Rico died before he could go to trial. In November 2008, Connolly was convicted by a Florida jury of second-degree murder in the death of Callahan. And now, Bulger himself will finally face charges in the case.

## THE 99 RESTAURANT & PUB HIT

*29–31 Austin Street, between Main Street and Rutherford Avenue, Charlestown*

It was a hit both horrific and hilarious, an out-of-nowhere explosion of violence that sent a lunch crowd diving for cover as one father-and-son team gunned

The 99 Restaurant in Charlestown was the scene of a brazen hit by a father/son killing team against another father and son on November 6, 1995. As a crowd of lunchtime diners watched in horror, Anthony Clemente Sr. and his son Damian gunned down five men in broad daylight, killing four of them. *Photo by Stephanie Schorow.*

down another. For years afterward, Boston area residents could not quite think of the specials at the 99 Restaurant & Pub in quite the same way.

On November 6, 1995, about 1:30 p.m., diners, including a pair of off-duty cops, were quietly finishing up their lunch in the 99 Restaurant & Pub in Charlestown, just a few blocks from the famed Bunker Hill Monument. In one booth, Robert C. "Bobby" Luisi Sr.; his son, Roman; their relatives, brothers Antonio and Richard Sarro; and a family friend, Anthony Pelosi Jr., were having a meal of chicken, soup and sandwiches. Bobby Luisi was an alleged bookie and loan shark in the North End, supposedly linked to the faction led by Francis "Cadillac Frank" Salemme. His son, Roman, was facing legal troubles after being charged with a double murder in Los Angeles in 1992.

Approaching them that day were Anthony P. Clemente Sr. and his son, Damian, and a friend, Vincent Perez. The Clementes would later claim that Luisi had been bullying Damian Clemente and that he feared for his life. The elder Clemente said he did what any father would do: he tried to negotiate peace for his son with Luisi, to no avail. On November 6, the elder Clemente got a frantic call from his son after he ran into the Luisi party at the 99 Restaurant. The elder Clemente arrived and approached the Luisi party with a 9mm pistol.

Clemente would claim later that he thought Roman was reaching for a gun and he started shooting. Damian would join his father, with his .45. Thirteen bullets later, Luisi and his son, Antonio Sarro and Pelosi were dying and Richard Sarro was wounded, his life saved when Anthony Clemente ran out of bullets.

Two Everett plainclothes police officers, lunching nearby, had their meal interrupted by gunfire and a spray of blood. They dashed after the shooters and managed to subdue Damian Clemente and Vincent Perez. Two Boston police officers in the area also ran to the scene. Anthony Clemente calmly walked away; he was arrested the next day.

The sole survivor of the shooting, Richard Sarro, at first identified the Clementes as the killers but later declined to testify, winning him a contempt of court charge. At their 1997 trial, the Clementes argued that they had acted in self-defense. The jury, however, apparently wondered why the elder Clemente followed a wounded Robert Luisi and shot him twice more. One juror told the *Boston Globe* she believed the elder Clemente "did the North End a favor. But two wrongs don't make a right." The Clementes were convicted of first-degree murder, while Perez was found not guilty. Both Clementes are serving life sentences. The 99 Restaurant in Charlestown is still open for business.

## TENEAN BEACH

*Dorchester, Massachusetts*

Boston Harbor really isn't well known for its beaches, but a small, sandy strip in Dorchester called Tenean Beach is notorious. Its reputation isn't due to free parking, an on-site playground or even its spectacular view of the downtown skyline. It's known instead as a burial spot for the Winter Hill Gang. In September 2000, authorities acting on a tip discovered bones belonging to Paul "Paulie" McGonagle, the leader of the Mullen Gang, buried on Tenean Beach. The sands kept McGonagle's body hidden for twenty years, but they couldn't hide the identity of his suspected killer. James "Whitey" Bulger, a rival of McGonagle, was believed to have iced the Irish mobster in November 1974 after McGonagle became enraged when Bulger killed his younger brother, Donald, in a case of mistaken identity. Not far from McGonagle's body, authorities also uncovered the remains of Debra Davis, the striking, blonde girlfriend of Stephen Flemmi who was strangled by Bulger in 1981 inside the basement of Flemmi's mother's house

Tenean Beach in Dorchester, where police dug up the bodies of three of Whitey Bulger's victims, including Debra Davis, the girlfriend of his accomplice Stephen "The Rifleman" Flemmi. Davis was killed because she supposedly "knew too much." *Photo by Beverly Ford.*

in South Boston. Flemmi would later tell investigators that Davis was murdered because she "knew too much" about the pair's criminal activities and status as FBI informants. Authorities would later dig up three more bodies nearby: John McIntyre, killed after he implicated the Bulger clan in a drug-smuggling and gunrunning operation; Arthur "Bucky" Barrett, who was involved in the 1980 Memorial Day weekend burglary of Depositors Trust in Medford; and Deborah Hussey, Flemmi's girlfriend and stepdaughter. The bodies of these three victims were found a short distance away from Tenean Beach near Florian Hall, a local union gathering spot in Dorchester. All had been first buried in the basement of a South Boston home by Bulger and Flemmi, who then exhumed the bodies in October 1985 when the house was put up for sale.

## The Tong Wars

*Chinatown, Boston*

Irish and Italians were not the only ethnic group in Boston to run a criminal underworld. Asian organized gangs, often called tongs, also left their mark

*Above*: Police commissioner Eugene Holtman and Superintendent Michael Crowley put up a poster in Chinese with warnings about the tongs, Chinese gangs that often engaged in lethal business transactions. *Courtesy of the Boston Public Library, Print Department.*

*Below*: A victim of the tong war in Boston's Chinatown. The victim, a male, was shot nine times in an alleyway. Police speculate the murderer had a silencer. *Courtesy of the Boston Public Library, Print Department.*

in the city, often under the radar of local authorities and the mainstream Boston press.

Boston's first tong war began with the October 2, 1903 murder of Wong Yak Chong, the thirty-year-old owner of a laundry in Boston's Roslindale neighborhood and a member of the Hip Sing Tong. Shot dead on Harrison Avenue in Boston's Chinatown neighborhood, Chong's death marked the first murder in Boston's Chinese community since the 1880s. His killers, however, weren't on the street long. Two Chinese men, one described as wearing a shirt of steel chainmail and carrying a hatchet, were arrested shortly after the shooting. Newspaper accounts said the men were "Highbinders," killers hired by the On Leong Tong to eliminate gang rivals, and warned of a pending "Highbinder War." In provocative, racially insensitive prose, newspaper articles at the time declared that "Wiley Mongolians," bent on murder and protected by Chinatown's secretive "hives," were on a mission for revenge, as correspondent Chris Berdick reported one hundred years later in a 2003 *Boston Globe* article.

The brutality of Chong's murder sent a shiver of fear throughout the city even though Chinatown residents had long warned police that violence was brewing. Fueled by sensational press coverage about a possible feud among Chinatown tongs, which controlled the neighborhood's illicit businesses such as gaming, Boston city officials decided that only a "close and constant espionage on the neighborhood" could prevent further bloodletting, Berdick wrote. Soon, the tenor of the press coverage ratcheted fear up a notch, with charged prose that described the blackmailing of illegal Chinese laborers and how police had determined that Chinatown's ills were caused by illegal immigrants.

Ten days after Chong was killed, an army of police and immigration officials, operating without warrants, began raiding restaurants, laundries and other Chinatown businesses, arresting every Asian male who could not produce the registration papers required of Chinese immigrants since 1892. By the next morning, the city's papers were reporting the arrest of three hundred Asian men in bold headlines across their front pages. Fifty of those men were deported. The remainder were released within days.

By the 1980s, crime in Boston's Asian communities was organized under the leadership of Stephen Tse, a Hong Kong native nicknamed "Sky Dragon." Arriving in Boston from New York City, Tse organized a gang composed largely of young, unskilled Asian immigrants. According to William Kleinknecht's book *The New Ethnic Mobs*, Tse incorporated his gang in 1982 as the Ping On Club, headquartered at 6 Tyler Street. Violence, including killings, soon followed. Eventually, Ping On seized control over gambling operations in Chinatown, later branching out into prostitution, loan-sharking, extortion and drugs. Tse was the unquestioned "Dai Lo," or big brother, of the gang. Though he lived outside Boston, in Braintree, he was said to rule Chinatown's criminal element. Businesses paid protection money to his gang, and immigrant families sometimes lost their livelihoods with one roll of the dice. But for several years, the streets remained largely free of violence. "When Stephen Tse was here, he was not called the 'Sky Dragon' for nothing," Bill Moy, co-moderator of the Chinatown Neighborhood Council, told the *Boston Globe*. "He kept things under control." That control slipped in the fall of 1984, when Tse was jailed for refusing to testify before a presidential commission on Asian organized crime. At the same time, the Ping On was facing new rivals in emerging Vietnamese gangs. After he was released from jail, Tse was forced to move back to Hong Kong in 1989 but was extradited back to the United States to face racketeering charges.

Then on January 12, 1991, rivalries erupted into a bloodbath that left five men dead and one clinging to life in a basement social club on Chinatown's Tyler Street. (See the following section.) The murders prompted an international manhunt and took more than a decade to solve.

Today, at least four gangs, including the Ping On, are said to be operating in the area's Asian communities.

## TYLER STREET MASSACRE

*85A Tyler Street, between Harrison Avenue and Hudson Street, near the corner of Kneeland Street, Chinatown, Boston*

Even during a year when Boston was enduring one of its highest homicide rates in history, the brutal slayings shocked a city and horrified the close-knit Asian community in Boston's Chinatown. Situated away from a main street lined with Chinese restaurants, street vendors and pagoda-topped telephone booths, Tyler Street was a quiet haven of brick apartment buildings and small street-front shops. At about 4:00 a.m. on January 12, 1991, as patrons played cards inside a social club at 85A Tyler Street, three men burst through the red front door shouting "robbery" and ordered everyone to the floor. Within minutes, five men were dead. Cuong Khanh Luu, twenty-six; Man Cheung, fifty-five; David Quang Lam, thirty-two; Chung Wah Son, fifty-eight; and Van Tran, thirty-one, were shot in the head at near point-blank range. One man, Pak Wing Lee, survived. He described how three men he knew from the neighborhood shot the men as they begged for their lives. Lee felt a gun being put to the back of his head, and then nothing. He was shot, but miraculously,

Tyler Street in Boston's Chinatown, where five people were massacred during a card game at an after-hours social club. The murders sparked an international manhunt. *Photo by Stephanie Schorow.*

the bullet did not pierce his brain. The club manager, known as "Wrinkled Skin Man," who told police he fled when the gunmen ran out of bullets, would eventually identify the suspects. "It's a real ugly scene down there," Mayor Raymond L. Flynn told reporters the next day. "It looks like a war scene."

Two of the three men suspected in the shootings were eventually tracked down in China and, after years of diplomatic haggling, were sent back to Boston to face trial. In 2005, fourteen years after the massacre, Siny Van Tran, known as "Toothless Wah," and Nam The Tham, known as "Johnny Cheung," both Vietnamese, were each found guilty of five counts of first-degree murder. Both men were sentenced to life in prison. The third suspect has not been found.

## FRANK WALLACE AND BARNEY "DODO" WALSH

*Testa Building, 317 Hanover Street*

Gustin Gang leader Frank Wallace, called to a meeting with Italian mobster Joseph Lombardo, was expecting to settle a dispute over bootlegging proceeds when he and enforcer Barney "Dodo" Walsh were cut down in a hail of

*Above*: The animosity between the Irish and Italian gangs reached a lethal boiling point in 1931, when Frank Wallace and two other men were shot in an office inside the Testa Building on Hanover Street in the North End. Wallace, leader of the notorious Gustin Gang, was meeting with Italian mobster Joseph Lombardo to discuss bootlegging business. Instead, a gunfight broke out, leaving Wallace and one of his enforcers, Barney "Dodo" Walsh, dead at the scene. Another victim, Timothy Coffey, survived by hiding in an office down the hall until police arrived. *Courtesy of the Boston Public Library, Print Department.*

*Left*: The Testa Building on Hanover Street in Boston's North End. The shooting ended the reign of the Gustin Gang. *Courtesy of the Boston Public Library, Print Department.*

The ground floor of the Testa Building on Hanover in the North End today. *Photo by Beverly Ford.*

bullets outside Lombardo's third-floor office. No one was ever convicted of the 1931 slayings. Today, the Testa building where the shooting occurred still stands on busy Hanover Street in Boston's North End, but few residents of the neighborhood are aware of its bloody history.

# Chapter 5
# TINSEL TOWNIES

## BOSTON MOBSTERS IN THE MOVIES

The Charlestown bank robber walks into a room where his buddy is watching TV. "I need your help. I can't tell you what it is. You can never ask me about it later. I'm gonna hurt some people," the robber says in a staccato growl. His friend barely hesitates. "Whose car are we gonna take?"

In a few words, this notorious snippet of dialogue from the movie *The Town* captures the mindset of Boston's underworld. Sure, the movie, directed by and starring Ben Affleck, was dramatically overblown, and its claim that Charlestown was the bank-robbing capital of the state was dubious, at least statistically. Nonetheless, *The Town*'s portrayal rings true about young thugs being manipulated by a cunning and cruel criminal puppet master, and the authors of this book can attest that Charlestown and Southie both take a perverse pride in their neighborhoods' criminal history.

It's been observed that after Francis Ford Coppola's *Godfather* series was released, wise guys began to imitate the mobsters they saw on the screen. Likewise, actors asked to play gangsters often hung out with wise guys, adapting their portrayals. By the time *The Sopranos* made its mark, the line between reality and fiction was even more blurred.

Boston's gangsters may lack a cinematic narrative with the majestic sweep of *The Godfather*, but the Hub's dark side has inspired a host of filmmakers, including Martin Scorsese and Affleck, who, despite his upbringing in affluent Cambridge, remains fascinated with the "townies" of Charlestown and Southie. Here, too, the line between fact and fantasy blurs. When Whitey Bulger was finally arrested, Jack Nicholson's portrayal of a Whitey-like criminal boss in *The Departed* was frequently cited by the media to explain just who Whitey was. The following is a summary (in order of importance) of a few of the most compelling films about Boston's mobsters that were, at least partly, filmed in Boston.

## THE FRIENDS OF EDDIE COYLE

*Directed by Peter Yates, 1973*

This is the undisputed king of all Boston gangland movies and probably one of the best films ever made about the working stiffs of the underworld. This study of wise guys at the bottom of the mobster ladder opens in the concrete wasteland of Boston's Government Center, a complex built on the site of the razed, raffish Scollay Square. The soulless setting is a backdrop to the cat and mouse game between a detective and his informant, and it takes the viewer a few minutes to figure out just who is who. Based closely on the

Robert Mitchum (left) gives the performance of his life as a lowlife crook facing a long jail sentences in *The Friends of Eddie Coyle*, based on the book by George V. Higgins. His speech to Jackie Brown (Steven Keats) on how he got the nickname "Fingers" is an iconic depiction of "business-as-usual" in Boston's underworld. *Paramount Pictures.*

Perhaps due to the lingering memories of the 1950 Brink's robbery, in which masks of Captain Marvel played a key role, grotesque masks seem to play a part in many movies about criminals in the Hub. In *The Friends of Eddie Coyle*, masked bank robbers hold family members of bank personnel hostage, forcing bankers to open up safes. It's hard to say who is behind the mask, but in a case of life imitating the movies, it may be Alex Rocco, aka Alexander "Bobo" Petricone, who plays the bank robber, Scalise. *Paramount Pictures*.

classic book by George V. Higgins, *The Friends of Eddie Coyle* focuses on the last days of Eddie "Fingers" Coyle, a small-time hood vaguely operating by his own set of standards, as he tries to find a way to avoid jail time to stay with his wife and kids.

As Eddie, Robert Mitchum gives one of his best performances, and his monologue about how he came to have his hand broken is perhaps the best summation of the pitfalls of a criminal life. Peter Boyle plays a bartender and sometimes friend to Eddie, who is also working as an informant on the side. Richard Jordan is Detective Dave Foley, who is working the mean streets for all their worth. As Jackie Brown, a long-haired, muscle car–driving wannabe, Steven Keats has a standout scene filmed along the Charles River in which he toys with two counterculture revolutionaries seeking to buy guns. But it's Mitchum as Eddie, with his sad-sack eyes, who catches our sympathy mixed with revulsion as Eddie breaks his own code to stay out of jail. The movie was filmed entirely on location in Boston, and scenes at the old Boston Garden, mixed with clips from a Bruins hockey game, add to the sense of reality. The robberies were filmed with pitiless precision on location at banks on Boston's South Shore. Alex Rocco, aka Alexander "Bobo" Petricone (see "Alexander F. Petricone Jr." page 66), plays the bank robber Jimmy Scalise, who holds bank managers' families hostage until the manager opens up the locks to the money. It's a smooth operation until a bank teller decides to be a hero and things get bloody. Meanwhile, Coyle plods along, never realizing his fate is sealed.

## THE DEPARTED

*Directed by Martin Scorsese, 2006*

Jack Nicholson's portrayal of Irish Boston mob boss Frank Costello was so compelling that when the real Whitey Bulger was arrested, *The Departed* was cited repeatedly as a fictionalized version of Bulger's saga. Actually, *The Departed*, which won the Academy Award for Best Motion Picture, is based on a Hong Kong action film, *Infernal Affairs*, but Nicholson's depiction of the sadist, unkempt but compelling Costello had many Bostonians wondering if Whitey himself had seen the movie while on the lam. (Rumors insist so.) Nonetheless, with its all-star crew, including native sons Matt Damon as a rogue FBI agent and Mark Wahlberg as the most incredibly foul-mouthed police investigator you'll ever meet, *The Departed* is director Martin Scorcese's vision of the evil sown by a charismatic criminal without a qualm in the world.

A jittery Leonardo DiCaprio plays state police officer Billy Costigan, who goes deep undercover to penetrate the organization run by Costello, seen early on coolly executing a young man and woman on what appears to be Tenean Beach in Dorchester, a site where Bulger's crew actually buried victims. DiCaprio is recruited by an avuncular Captain Oliver Queenan (Martin Sheen, channeling a role he also played in *Monument Ave.*) and expletive-spewing Sergeant Dignam (Wahlberg). Costigan is told that Costello has someone within the FBI feeding him information and protecting him. That someone, Colin Sullivan (a suave Damon), revels in his dual role as up-and-coming special investigator and underworld conduit. Sullivan's apartment has a view of the golden dome of the Boston State House, representing the prestige and power to which Sullivan aspired—or perhaps a reference to the career of William "Billy" Bulger, Whitey's brother. Boston scenes include a ride over the Zakim Bunker Hill Bridge and a confrontation

Jack Nicholson (left) gives such a mesmerizing portrait of mobster Frank Costello—based on James "Whitey" Bulger—in the movie *The Departed* that when the real Whitey was arrested, Nicholson's performance was cited. A jittery, ragged Leonardo DiCaprio (right) plays a state police officer on deep cover who has penetrated Costello's organization, and Matt Damon plays a clean-cut, promising FBI man who is actually protecting Costello, a role inspired by FBI agent John Connolly. *Warner Bros. Pictures*.

on Boston's harbor front between Costello and the state police authorities, Dignam and Queenan. Queenan meets a grisly fate in a sequence that uses a warehouse section in the Fort Point Channel neighborhood in South Boston as a backdrop. The movie has a gritty, unsettled feeling and ends in a series of bloodbaths, each more shocking than the last. The movie quickly departs from the facts of Whitey's life but captures the uneasy alliances made in the name of profit and justice.

## THE TOWN

*Directed by Ben Affleck, 2010*

You can take the boy out of Boston, but you can't take Boston out of the boy. Ben Affleck starred in and directed this slice of Boston's street life. *The Town* opens with the assertion that "there are over three hundred bank robberies

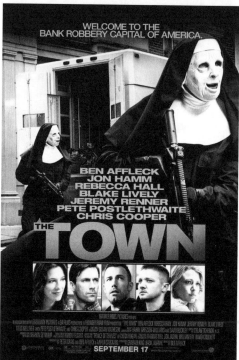

*Above*: In a scene filmed at the famed ballpark, robbers played by Ben Affleck and Jeremy Renner prepare to pull off the heist of their life at Fenway Park in *The Town*. The scene is wildly preposterous, and the movie's portrayal of Charlestown as the bank-robbing capital of the country is wildly overblown, yet *The Town* gives a sense of a community that operates in the shadows, living only for the next score. The chase scenes in Boston's North End are worth the price of admission. *Warner Bros. Pictures*.

*Left*: Again with the masks! The grotesque masks and nuns' habits are a reoccurring motif in publicity for *The Town*, starring Ben Affleck as a bank robber who falls in love with one of his victims. Note the slogan in this movie poster. *Warner Bros. Pictures*.

in Boston every year. Most of these professionals live in a one-square-mile neighborhood called Charlestown." Whether this is statistically true is beside the point. Affleck plays Doug McRay, who, with best friend James Couglin (Jeremy Renner) and other buddies, pulls off daring robberies with careful planning and precision (the robberies unapologetically reference *The Friends of Eddie Coyle*, and the masks used could be leftover props from *The Brink's Job*). A bank manager is accidentally taken hostage and released, and after he learns that she lives in Charlestown, Doug befriends her to find what she knows. Predictably, he falls in love and is torn between loyalties. Perhaps the most notable scene filmed in Boston is an improbable chase through the narrow streets of the city's North End. A robbery at Fenway Park is pure fantasy, a mash-up of obsessions, and ends tragically for the Charlestown characters.

## MONUMENT AVE.

*Directed by Ted Demme, 1998*

In Charlestown, under the shadow of that sacred American icon, the Bunker Hill Monument, a group of young Charlestown goofs scampers up Monument Avenue, setting off car alarms just for the hell of it. Boston comedian Denis Leary, talking rapid-fire in a barely comprehensible accent, plays Bobby O'Grady, a small-time hoodlum who views car jacking as a good

Monument Avenue in Charlestown, the place that was once reputed to have produced more bank robbers than any other place in the nation. *Monument Avenue* is also the name of a 1998 movie starring Denis Leary that highlighted the closed-mouth culture of Boston's Irish underworld. *Photo by Stephanie Schorow.*

career path. Bobby gets a stinging wake-up call when his talkative cousin (Billy Crudup) is shot to death in front of him on orders from Irish mob boss Jackie O'Hara (Colm Meaney), who knows no one will break the Irish code of silence. (Not even if the detective is played by Martin Sheen, who sneers at everyone's favorite excuse: "I was in the bathroom when it happened.") Jackie may be a sadistic thug, but he also doles out money and favors to the community, a mayor of mayhem who keeps in line both young bucks like Bobby and weary grannies. O'Grady begins to realize the price that's paid for "being in the bathroom." Filmed on location with local comedians such as Lenny Clark, *Monument Ave.* was another salvo in exposing the rotting underside of "Robin Hood" bosses like Whitey Bulger, then four years into his "exile."

# THE BRINK'S JOB

*Directed by William Friedkin, 1978*

William Friedkin (*The Exorcist, The French Connection*) views the story of the 1950 robbery of the Brink's armored car service in Boston's North End as a classic celebration of the little guy. The "little guy" in this case was Tony Pino (Peter Falk), the mastermind of the heist and a compulsive thief who saw the robbery as his masterpiece. Peter Falk bears little resemblance to the real Tony Pino, whose bulk led to his nickname of "Fats," but he captures his single-minded determination to pull off what would be the largest robbery in U.S. history to date. Perhaps the best scene is the tête-à-tête between Pino and his wife filmed at Doyle's, the popular restaurant in Boston's Jamaica Plain neighborhood. The money in the Brink's headquarters is speaking to him, Pino says. "Tony, come and get me. Get me out of here." So Pino organizes his crew—a scary Peter Boyle as bartender Joe McGinnis, Paul Sorvino as a dapper Jazz Maffie, Gerard Murphy as Sandy Richardson, Allen Goorwitz as goofball Vinnie Costa and a twitchy Warren Oates as turncoat Specky O'Keefe. Sheldon Leonard does a marvelous portrayal of FBI director J. Edgar Hoover, capturing in a few lines Hoover's power and arrogance. The movie, while based on a nonfiction book by Noel Behn, plays fast and loose with the facts of the case, yet there is an aura of truth to it. For starters, the robbery is filmed at the actual scene of the crime. Brink's had long departed from the North Terminal Garage in the North End so the filmmakers took it over and rebuilt the offices, including finding and

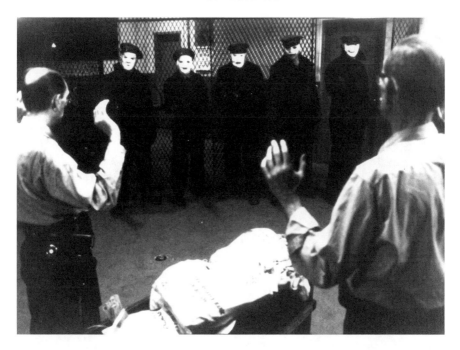

For the movie *The Brink's Job*, filmmakers re-created the 1950 heist on location in the North Terminal Garage in the North End, the former headquarters of the Brink's armored car company in Boston. *Universal Studios.*

returning the actual door to the vault. Filmmakers wanted to use a section of East Boston for a scene set in the 1930s and offered to pay residents to take their air conditioning units out for the shot. Wouldn't you know it? By the next day, air conditioning units had sprung up in windows like toadstools after a rain; the residents very kindly offered to take them out for the promised fee. Friedkin retained the living Brink's robbers, notably Sandy Richardson and Jazz Maffie, as consultants. When the movie was released in 1978, Mayor Kevin White declared "Brink's Week" in Boston, and the robbers were treated like honored celebrities.

## SIX BRIDGES TO CROSS

*Directed by Joseph Pevney, 1955*

Despite its all-star cast, including a blissfully young Tony Curtis, and theme song sung by Sammy Davis Jr., *Six Bridges to Cross* did not make a big splash when it was released in 1955. Yet it could have won an award for best

A masked Tony Curtis, in a role based on Brink's robbery mastermind Tony Pino, stages a holdup in the 1954 movie *Six Bridges to Cross*, which featured numerous Boston locations. The movie contains an eerily accurate depiction of the 1950 Brink's robbery—all the more amazing as the film was made before any of the robbers were brought to justice and the case "solved." The dispatcher shown in the movie announcing the robbery was a police dispatcher who made the actual call on the night of January 17, 1950, when Brink's guards managed to call police. *Universal Pictures Company.*

speculation: the scenes inspired by the Brink's robbery were close to the fact—even though the crime would not be officially solved for another year. Based on the novel *The Anatomy of a Crime* by *Boston Globe* scribe Joseph F. Dinneen (who reputedly made more money writing about the Brink's robbery than any of the individual robbers made), *Six Bridges* begins with petty mischief by a young Jerry Florea (played with impish winning charm by Sal Mineo), who graduates to more serious crimes. A rookie cop, Eddie Gallagher (George Nader), and his wife (Julia Adams) try to turn Jerry to a more respectable life. But Jerry, played by Curtis as an adult, can't give up the glamour of a gangster's life, and he ends up masterminding a heist at "Doane's Transfer." There's a sneaky subtext here: Mineo and then Curtis are so engaging, funny and lively that you can't help rooting for him over Gallagher's staid, Dragnet-esque "good guy." Filmed in Boston with evocative scenes of a 1950s Hub, *Six*

*Bridges* features the police dispatcher who took the original call on the Brink's robbery reprising his words for the camera. Tony Curtis would "return" to Boston with a mesmerizing turn as the lead in *The Boston Strangler*, the 1968 movie also filmed on location.

# MYSTIC RIVER

*Directed by Clint Eastwood, 2003*

Few lines in Boston cinema are as chilling as the seductive words spoken to Jimmy Markum (Sean Penn), a supposedly "retired" criminal who has taken misguided revenge for his daughter's murder. "Everyone else is weak, Jimmy. Everyone but us," coos his wife, Annabeth (Laura Linney). "We will never be weak. And you...You could rule this town." The lines seem to come out of nowhere in this mystery thriller that focuses on three childhood friends, but it only underscores a basic tenet of Boston's mob world: morality is a nicety no wise guy can afford. The Clint Eastwood–directed version of Dennis Lehane's popular novel begins with three youngsters—Jimmy Markum, Dave Boyle and Sean Devine—playing in the streets of a Boston neighborhood when, by a twist of fate, young Dave is kidnapped by pedophiles. Years later, Boyle (Tim Robbins) is a broken man, Markum is an ex-con now running a grocery store and still commanding respect among the criminals he used to lead, and Devine (Kevin Bacon) is a detective. Markum's daughter is found murdered, and the ghosts of the past emerge to claim fresh victims. Scenes were shot all over Boston—at Doyle's Café in Jamaica Plain, K Street in South Boston and Condor Street in East Boston, among others.

# AFTERWORD

*On one hand, John Martorano has done great harm, but on the other he has played an important role in bringing to light an even greater evil.*
*—letter written by David Wheeler, son of slain businessman Roger Wheeler, to U.S. District judge Mark L. Wolf in 2004 when Martorano was sentenced*

In July 2009, reputed New England Mafia underboss Carmen "The Cheese Man" DiNunzio pleaded guilty to a host of charges, including extortion, illegal gambling and bribery charges. He was sentenced to six years in prison. DiNunzio, a balding man with gargantuan proportions, got his nickname for owning the Fresh Cheese Shop on Endicott Street in the North End, but it also reflected on his girth. Mob watchers shook their head; the bland Cheese Man seemed to be a far cry from the bosses of yore. Two years later, after another arrest of a small-fry mobster, *Boston Globe* writer Kevin Cullen did a metaphorical dance on the grave of Boston's underworld. "The Mafia around here sleeps with the fishes," Cullen wrote on October 24, 2010. "It's over. Finito. Like that last scene from *The Sopranos*. Fade to black."

It would be going too far to conclude that organized crime in Boston has disappeared. Bank robberies go on, drug deals are done and too many young men and women are dying in gang-related violence in poorer neighborhoods—Asian, Latin and African American, as well as Irish and Italians—often with innocents caught in the crossfire. Corruption continues, sometimes on the streets, sometimes in municipal offices.

Headlines herald the capture of Whitey Bulger in June 2011 after Bulger eluded capture for sixteen years. Many cynical Bostonians wonder if the FBI really wanted to capture the gangster who had once been an FBI informant. *Composite by Stephanie Schorow.*

What is most disturbing about Boston's mob saga is the complicity of authorities. We've detailed the actions of the FBI's H. Paul Rico and John Connolly, who looked the other way as their informants committed murders, but there were others. And then there's the apathy of the community and of the press, who figure that as long as the bad guys (often from a minority group) are just killing each other off, what's the harm? Nothing—unless you are the wife, child, mother or father of a victim or an innocent bystander caught in the crossfire.

Yet it is clear that the capture of Whitey Bulger represents the end of an era for Boston's underworld. Authorities are "chasing old men in diapers," Rhode Island defense attorney Raymond Mansolillo told Laura Crimaldi of the Associated Press a few days after an aging Whitey was apprehended in June 2011. While there are still lingering mysteries, perhaps some of them will be cleared up when—and if—Bulger ever takes the stand in court.

Despite the undeniable fascination generated by Boston's crime bosses, few will be sad to see their era ended.

# SOURCES

The material in this book is drawn from published sources, including issues of the *Boston Herald, Boston Globe, New York Times, Providence Journal,* the Associated Press and other New England newspapers from the 1920s to today; books written about Boston's mob and by mobsters; websites devoted to organized crime; the authors' own research; and interviews from their years as reporters and writers. It should be noted that mobsters (and often news reporters) can be unreliable narrators, but the authors have made every effort to stick to known and established facts about the cases described in these pages, even if that means omitting a colorful story.

## BOOKS

Atkinson, Jay. *Legends of Winter Hill: Cops, Con Men, and Joe McCain, the Last Real Detective.* New York: Three Rivers Press, 2006.

Carr, Howie. *The Brothers Bulger: How They Terrorized and Corrupted Boston for a Quarter Century.* New York: Grand Central Publishing, 2006

———. *Hitman: The Untold Story of Johnny Martorano: Whitey Bulger's Enforcer and the Most Feared Gangster in the Underworld.* New York: Forge, 2011.

# SOURCES

English, T.J. *Paddy Whacked: The Untold Story of the Irish-American Gangster.* New York: William Morrow, 2005.

Kleinknecht, William. *The New Ethnic Mobs: The Changing Face of Organized Crime in America.* New York: Free Press, 1996.

Lehr, Dick, and Gerard O'Neill. *Black Mass: The True Story of an Unholy Alliance Between the FBI and the Irish Mob.* New York: PublicAffairs, 2000.

————. *The Underboss: The Rise and Fall of a Mafia Family.* New York: Perennial, 2001.

MacKenzie Edward J., Jr., and Phyllis Kara. *Street Soldier: My Life as an Enforcer for Whitey Bulger and the Boston Irish Mob.* South Royalton, VT: Steerforth Press, 2003.

Martini, Bobby, with Elayne Keratsis. *Citizen Somerville: Growing Up with the Winter Hill Gang.* North Reading, MA: Power House Press, 2010.

Shea, John "Red." *Rat Bastards: The Life and Times of South Boston's Most Honorable Irish Mobster: A Memoir.* New York: William Morrow, 2006.

Teresa, Vincent Charles. *My Life in the Mafia.* Cutchogue, NY: Buccaneer Books, 1994.

Weeks, Kevin, and Phyllis Karas. *Brutal: The Untold Story of My Life Inside Whitey Bulger's Irish Mob.* New York: HarperCollins, 2006.

# WEBSITES

The American Mafia: The History of Organized Crime in the United States. www.onewal.com.

The Crime Library. www.trutv.com/library/crime/gangsters_outlaws/index.html.

Internet Movie Data Base. www.imdb.com.

Rick Porrello's American Mafia.com. www.americanmafia.com.

# INDEX

## A

Adams, Julia 146
Adams Street 40
Affleck, Ben 137, 141, 143
Alcatraz 17
Alpert, Mickey 98
Angiulo, Ceasar 25, 32
Angiulo, Donato 31, 32,
    96, 102
Angiulo, Francesco "Frank"
    31, 32
Angiulo, Gennaro "Jerry"
    9, 20, 25, 26, 27,
    28, 30, 35, 36, 37,
    47, 62, 63, 65, 72,
    75, 90, 91, 93, 95,
    97, 101
Angiulo, Giovannina 25, 32
Angiulo, James "Jimmy
    Jones" 31
Angiulo, Michele "Mickey"
    31, 33
Angiulo, Vittore Nicolo
    "Nicky" 31, 33
Anthony's Pier 4 restaurant
    87, 119, 120
Arlington Street 117
AtlantiCare Medical
    Hospital 74
Audi 68
Auerhahn, Jeffrey 43
Austin Street 126

## B

Back Bay 40, 43
Baker, Henry 115, 117
Banfield, Barney 115
Barboza, Joseph "the
    Animal" 9, 27, 28,
    34, 35, 36, 37, 45,
    63, 64, 69, 71, 72,
    74, 75, 92, 112, 113,
    118, 123, 124
Barrett, Arthur "Bucky"
    97, 119, 129
Barrett, Douglas 55
Basin Street South 55
*Batman* 68
Baxter, Thomas F. 13
Beacon Hill 97
Beatty, Jack 61, 62
Belmont, Massachusetts 68
Benjamin, Frank 122
Bennett, Edward "Wimpy"
    109, 116, 117
Bennett, Walter 109, 110
Bennett, William "Billy"
    109, 110
Berdick, Chris 131
Bianco, Nicholas "Nicky"
    65, 66, 75
bin Laden, Osama 13
Blackfriars 11, 111, 112
*Black Mass* 16
Blythe, Michael 60
BMW 74

Boston Bruins 20
Boston Celtics 20
Boston Charlie 81
Boston College 53, 69, 99
Boston English High School
    25
Boston Garden 20, 139
*Boston Globe* 10, 40, 49, 55,
    57, 65, 68, 79, 88,
    92, 109, 111, 114,
    128, 131, 132, 146,
    149, 160
Boston Harbor 14, 28, 122,
    128
*Boston Herald* 7, 10, 17, 43,
    56, 91, 160
Boston Police Department
    23
Braintree, Massachusetts
    38, 132
Bratsos, Arthur "Tash" 35,
    36, 112, 113
Breen, David J. "Beano" 98
Brink's 10, 11, 40, 97, 109,
    113, 114, 115, 116,
    117, 143, 144, 145,
    146, 147
*Brink's Job, The* 117, 143,
    144
Broadway 57, 84, 85, 104,
    122, 124
Brooke, Edward W. 27
Brookline, Massachusetts
    61, 64, 76, 79, 110

Brunswick Street 55
Buccelli, John F. "Fats" 116, 117
Buccigross, James 99
Buccola, (Bruccola) Filippo 38, 50, 60
Bulger, James J. "Whitey" 9, 10, 11, 12, 13, 14, 15, 16, 17, 18, 19, 20, 21, 22, 23, 29, 31, 32, 41, 42, 46, 47, 48, 54, 55, 56, 60, 69, 70, 75, 76, 85, 87, 88, 90, 91, 100, 105, 106, 107, 119, 120, 125, 126, 128, 129, 140, 144, 150
Bulger, William "Billy" 10, 18
Bunker Hill Monument 127, 143
Burke, Elmer Francis 39, 40, 97, 114, 116
Byrne, Garrett H. 48, 99, 116, 117

**C**

Cadillac 21, 30, 72, 113, 126
Café Pompeii 32, 96
Cagney, James 76
Callahan, John 21, 22, 125, 126
Cameron, William 116
Candos, Robert 64
Carlson, John Henry "Johnny" 116
Carr, Howie 17, 43, 56, 91
Carrozza, Robert F. 66, 74
Castellammarese War 60
Castle Island 11, 14, 96
Castle Square 117
Castro, Fidel 64
Castucci, Richard J. 55
Cavanaugh, William E. 40
C&F Importing 83
Chandler's Restaurant 60, 97
Chandler, Willard M. 97
Charles Street 40, 97
Charles Street jail 40, 97

Charlestown 11, 14, 45, 56, 57, 58, 68, 74, 89, 120, 122, 124, 126, 128, 137, 143
Chelsea, Massachusetts 69, 118
Cheung, Johnny 133
Cheung, Man 132
Chinatown 129, 131, 132
Chinatown Neighborhood Council 132
Chong, Wong Yak 131
*Citizen Somerville: Growing Up with the Winter Hill Gang* 90
City Square, Charlestown 57, 122
Ciulla, "Fat Tony" 19
Clemente, Anthony P. 127, 128
Clemente, Damian 127, 128
Clemente, Gerald W. 119
Coakley, Daniel 62
Coast Guard 28
Cocoanut Grove nightclub 9, 10, 76, 78, 79, 81, 98, 99
Coffey, Timothy 83
Coin-O-Matic Distributing Company 63
Colombo crime family 66
Columbus Avenue 97
Combat Zone 27, 30, 35, 54, 102
Commercial Street 30, 112, 113, 114
Condon, Dennis 64
Connecticut River 74
Connelly, Richard 111
Connolly, John 15, 16, 20, 22, 23, 41, 42, 53, 56, 58, 75, 76, 85, 88, 91, 106, 120, 126, 150
Connors, Eddie 55
*Cops Are Robbers, The* 119
Costa, Vincent James 114, 115, 117, 144
Cotton Club 76, 79, 81, 98
Coyne, James J. "Skeets" 81
Crimaldi, Laura 150
*Criminal and an Irishman: The Inside Story of*

*the Boston Mob-IRA Connection, A* 60
Crocket, Douglas S. 111
Crudup, Billy 144
Cucchiara, Frank 59
Cullen, Kevin 65, 149
Curcio, Raymond "Baby" 64
Curley, James Michael 61
Curtis, Tony 145, 146, 147

**D**

Daddieco, Robert 110
Dai Lo 132
Damon, Matt 140
Danvers, Massachusetts 116
David L. Moss Criminal Justice Center 70
Davis, Debra 47, 128
Deady, Philip 99
Deegan, Edward "Teddy" 37, 48, 69, 70, 118
Deer Island 109, 117
Delavega, Freddy R. 111
Deluca, Robert P. 66
*Departed, The* 23, 138, 140
Depositors Trust Bank 119
DePrisco, Thomas J. 35, 112, 113
Dermondy, Ronald 122, 123
*Detroit News* 83
Devens, Massachusetts 30
DiCaprio, Leonardo 140
Dickson, Elizabeth 55
DiGiacomo, Biagio 66
Dinneen, Joseph F. 114, 146
DiNunzio, Carmen "The Cheese Man" 149
DiSarro, Steve 76
Donahue, Michael 87, 119, 120
Dorchester, Massachusetts 13, 14, 18, 28, 40, 55, 109, 110, 116, 119, 128, 129, 140
Dover Street 78
Downtown Crossing 11, 111
Drug Enforcement Administration 23, 52, 53
Dudley Street, Roxbury 110

# INDEX

## E

East Boston 34, 38, 56, 71, 112, 145, 147
East Second Street, South Boston 102
East Third Street, South Boston 43, 47, 100, 119
Endicott Street 149
England, Dorothy 79
English, T.J. 56

## F

Faherty, James Ignatius "Jimma" 115, 116
Falk, Peter 144
*Famous Teddy Z, The* 68
Fargo Building 116
Farrell, Richard 60
Father Fagin 62
Federal Bureau of Investigation (FBI) 13, 15, 20, 23, 24, 27, 28, 30, 32, 36, 41, 42, 43, 45, 46, 47, 48, 53, 58, 62, 63, 64, 68, 69, 70, 71, 72, 75, 76, 85, 88, 91, 95, 100, 101, 103, 106, 110, 114, 115, 118, 120, 126, 140, 144, 150
Federal Hill 63
Federico, Vincent 66, 71
Ferrara, Vincent "The Animal" 42, 43, 66, 74
Fitzgerald, John 37, 45, 75, 92
Flemmi, Stephen "the Rifleman" 9, 11, 19, 20, 22, 29, 30, 32, 35, 36, 42, 43, 44, 45, 46, 47, 48, 54, 55, 56, 63, 69, 70, 75, 76, 87, 88, 91, 100, 105, 109, 110, 119, 126, 128, 129

Flemmi, Vincent "Jimmy the Bear" 48, 69, 118, 122
Floramo, Richard J.E. 66
Flynn, James 87, 120
Flynn, Raymond L. 133
Framingham, Massachusetts 19, 125
Francesco's Restaurant 30, 101
Franklin High School 91
Franklin, Massachusetts 90
Franklin Park 116
Fresh Cheese Shop 149
Friedkin, William 144, 145
*Friends of Eddie Coyle, The* 68, 138, 139, 143
Fuller Street 79

## G

Gambino crime family 65
Garo, Victor 69, 118
Gasko, Charles 13
Geagan, Vincent 115
Genovese crime family 63, 65
G. Messina & Co. 59
*Godfather, The* 68, 137
Golini Drive 61
Grasso, Richard 110
Grasso, William P. 74
Greco, Louis 69, 118
Green, Moe 68
Greenstone, Leonard 81
Greig, Catherine 19, 23, 24, 88
Guglielmetti, Matthew 66
Guild Street, Medford, Massachusetts 71
Guinan, Texas 76, 78
Gusciora, Stanley "Gus" 114, 115
Gustin gang 9, 11, 38, 50, 51, 81, 83, 84, 85, 133

## H

Halloran, Brian 42, 87, 106, 119, 120, 126
Hanover Street 25, 31, 32, 50, 51, 83, 96, 113, 133, 135

Harbor Point Housing project 15
Harrison Avenue 131, 132
Harris, Tom 13
Harvard Street 109, 110
Higgins, George V. 139
Highbinder War 131
High Street 119
Hip Sing Tong 131
Holy Cross 99
Hong Kong 131, 132, 140
Hoover, J. Edgar 27, 62, 63, 144
Hopkinton Sportsmen's Association 110
Hudson Street 132
Hughes, Connie 58, 74, 124
Hughes, Stevie 58, 74, 124
Hull Street 114
Hurley, Charles F. 61, 62
Hussey, Deborah 22, 47, 119, 129

## I

Ierardi, William N. 112
International House of Pancakes 74
Irish mob wars 18, 48, 74, 89, 120
Italian-American Civil Rights League 65, 66
Italiano, Robert J. 112

## J

Jackson, John W. 55
Jacques Street 66
Jamaica Plain 40, 74, 111, 144, 147
Jay's Lounge 27, 101
John Joseph Mullen Square 102
Johnston, Rhode Island 61
Justice Department 23, 43

## K

Karas, Phyllis 88
Keats, Steven 139
Kefauver, C. Estes 27

Kelly, John A. "Jack" 111
Kennedy, Robert F. 62
Kiley, Edward 57
Killeen 11, 18, 19, 60, 97, 102, 125
Killeen, Donald 18, 19, 125
King, Tommy 55, 60, 105
Kleinknecht, William 131
Kneeland Street 132
Knights of Columbus Hall 102

**L**

La Cosa Nostra 32, 38, 62, 72, 91, 125
Lake, Austen 78, 81, 99
Lam, David Quang 132
Lancaster Foreign Car Service 20
Lancaster Street Garage 103
Landers, John 7
Latif, Louis 20, 107, 119, 120
Leary, Denis 143
Leavenworth Federal Penitentiary 17
Lee, Pak Wing 132
Lehr, Dick 16, 50, 51, 63
Lewisburg Federal Penitentiary 17
Lewis, Maurice 111
Liberty Hotel 40, 97
Limone, Peter 37, 69, 70, 118
Lincoln, Rhode Island 65
Locke, Allen G. 40
Lombardo, Joseph 9, 11, 26, 27, 38, 50, 51, 83, 133, 135
Luciano, Lucky 76
Luisi, Robert C. "Bobby" 127, 128
Luisi, Roman 127, 128
Lulu White's Jazz Club 97
Lumber Street 110
Luu, Cuong Khanh 132
Lynn, Massachusetts 74, 92

**M**

Maffie, Adolph "Jazz" 115, 117, 144, 145
Magarian, Charles G. 111

Mansolillo, Raymond 150
Maren, Tommy 79
Marfeo, Willie 64
Marino, Vincent Michael 51, 52, 53
Marshall Motors 20, 104
Marshall Street, Somerville 57, 104, 105
Marshall, Thomas 13
Martini, Bobby 90
Martorano, James 53, 97, 111
Martorano, John 20, 21, 22, 48, 54, 55, 56, 70, 88, 97, 105, 110, 126, 149
Mary Ellen McCormick Housing Project 14
Massachusetts attorney general 27
Massachusetts Bar Council 43
Massachusetts General Hospital 97
Massachusetts Governor's Council 61
Massachusetts State Police 23, 61, 88
May, Allan 61, 74
McConnell, Charles 52
McGinnis, Joe 114, 115, 116, 117, 144
McGonagle 18, 19, 128
McGonagle, Paul 18, 19, 128
McIntyre, John 22, 119, 129
McLaughlin, Bernie 57, 68, 122, 124
McLaughlin, Edward "Punchy" 70, 122, 124
McLaughlin, George 57, 68, 120, 122, 123, 124
McLean, Buddy 10, 11, 56, 57, 68, 89, 122, 123, 124
Meaney, Colm 144
Medford 43, 58, 65, 66, 71, 118, 119, 129
Medford Square 55, 119
Mercedes 30
Mercurio, Angelo "Sonny" 58, 66
Meroth, Peter 111

Merrimack Street, Boston 103
Messina, Gaspare 38, 58, 60
Messina, Gasparina 59
Messina, Giovanna 59
Messina, Luciano 59
Messina, Salvatore 59
Messina, Vito 59
Metropolitan Hotel 98
Miami Shores, Florida 68
Middleton, Massachusetts 125
Mineo, Sal 146
Mitchum, Robert 139
*Monument Ave.* 140, 143, 144
Morelli, Frank 38
Morelli Gang 38
Morris, John 20, 42
Morrissey Boulevard 55
most wanted list 24, 115
Moy, Bill 132
Mullen Gang 11, 18, 60, 97, 102, 125, 128
Murder Inc. 76
*My Life in the Mob* 68

**N**

Nader, George 146
Nahant, Massachusetts 25, 51
Nee, Patrick 60
Nelson, David 33
Neponset River Bridge 105
Neptune Oil Corporation 59
*New Ethnic Mobs, The* 131
New York City 39, 45, 84, 131
Nicholson, Jack 137, 140
Nicholson, Russell 122
Nimoy, Leonard 68
99 Restaurant & Pub 126
Nite Lite Café 36, 112
Normandy Street 55
North Andover 111
North End 9, 11, 14, 25, 26, 28, 30, 31, 33, 36, 42, 50, 51, 59, 65, 74, 81, 83, 84, 91, 93, 96, 102, 103, 113, 127, 128, 135, 143, 144, 149
Northern Avenue 119
North Margin Street 102

North Terminal Garage 11, 113, 114, 144
North Washington Street 30, 101
Notarageli, Joseph J. 55

**O**

O'Brien, Carlton 62, 116
O'Brien, George D. 116
O'Callahan Way 15
O'Keefe, Joseph James "Specky" 40, 114, 115, 116, 117, 144
Old Colony Avenue 105
Old Colony Housing project 15, 85
O'Neill, Gerard 16, 50, 51, 63
On Leong Tong 131
O Street, South Boston 102
O'Sullivan, Billy 18
O'Toole, James "Spike" 55
Owl Station Bar and Bistro 107

**P**

Pagnotta, Paolo 59
Pal Joey's 105
Palladino, Robert 55
Patriarca, Raymond "Junior" 58, 65, 66, 72, 75
Patriarca, Raymond L. S., Sr. 27, 38, 61, 62, 63, 64, 65, 75, 91, 116, 118
Patrizzi, Angelo 91
Pearl Harbor 25
Pelosi, Anthony 127
Perez, Vincent 127, 128
Petricone, Alexander F. 66, 68, 120, 140
Piedmont Street 98, 99
Ping On Club 131
Pino, Anthony 40, 114, 115, 116, 117, 144
Pleasure Bay 97, 102
Ponzi, Charles 99
Ponzi, Rose Gnecco 99
Portalla, "Gigi".

*See* Marino, Vincent Michael
Poulos, Peter 45, 46, 110
Prince Street 11, 20, 25, 28, 31, 32, 33, 47, 59, 91, 93, 95, 114
Profaci/Colombo crime families 63
Prohibition 10, 38, 59, 61, 81, 83
Providence, Rhode Island 27, 38, 61, 62, 63, 64, 65, 75, 118

**Q**

Quincy 41, 85, 105, 119
Quintina, Charles 66

**R**

Rakes, Julie 106
Rakes, Stephen 106
Rand, Sally 76
*Rascal King, The* 62
Renard, Jacques 98
Renner, Jeremy 143
Revere 17, 42, 52, 118, 124
Rhode Island 61
Richardson, Thomas Francis "Sandy" 114, 115, 116, 117, 144, 145
Rico, H. Paul 45, 46, 64, 68, 69, 70, 110, 118, 126, 150
Rocco, Alex. *See* Petricone, Alexander F., Jr.
Rolls Royce 30
Romney, Mitt 18
Roslindale 131
Roy, Teddy 77
Russo, Joseph "J.R." 37, 66, 71, 72, 74, 75, 92
Rutherford Avenue 126

**S**

Sacco, Nicola 38
Sagansky, Harry "Doc Jasper" 43

Salem, Massachusetts 77
Salemme, Francis "Cadillac Frank" 9, 44, 45, 46, 52, 56, 65, 66, 69, 72, 74, 75, 76, 110, 111, 127
Salvati, Joseph 69, 70, 118
San Francisco, California 17, 23, 34, 37, 64, 71, 92
Santa Monica 9, 13, 14, 24, 88
Sarro, Antonio 128
Sarro, Richard 127, 128
Saugus, Massachusetts 52, 74
Sewall Street 58
Shapeton, Mark 13
Shapiro, Frank 99
Shawmut Street 98
Shays, Christopher 70
Sheen, Martin 140, 144
Sheridan, William 122, 124
Shields, Hugh J. "Sonny" 110
*Simpsons, The* 68
*Six Bridges to Cross* 145
Sky Dragon 131, 132
Smith, Herbert "Smitty" 55
Smith, Paul 116
Snowhill Avenue 114
Solmonte, Vincent 111
Solomon, Bertha "Billie" 79
Solomon, Charles "King" 9, 10, 38, 76, 78, 79, 81, 98, 99
Solomon, Golda 77
Solomon, Joe 79
Solomon, Sarah Blum 77
Somerville 11, 20, 56, 57, 58, 60, 66, 68, 89, 104, 111, 120, 124
Son, Chung Wah 132
*Sopranos, The* 137, 149
South Boston 9, 11, 13, 14, 15, 17, 18, 19, 20, 22, 36, 41, 43, 44, 45, 47, 60, 81, 84, 85, 87, 88, 89, 96, 97, 100, 102, 106, 107, 110, 113, 116, 119, 125, 126, 129, 141, 147

South Boston Liquor Mart 23, 105
South End 14, 60, 90, 91, 97, 98, 116, 117
Southie 14, 15, 60, 81, 83, 88, 106, 107, 113, 137
Springfield, Missouri 71, 72, 90, 92
Stanley, Theresa 23, 114
St. Anthony de Padua Society 33
Stern, Donald 53
Stippo's Liquor Mart 106
St. Mary's Chapel 33
St. Monica's Church 15, 106
Suffolk County Jail 40, 97
Sullivan, Jerome 117
Summer Street 111, 116
Super Bowl 68
Sylvester, Margaret 53

**T**

Tailboard Thieves 81
Tameleo, Enrico 64
Tameleo, Henry 35, 37, 69, 118
Telex Corp. 70, 126
Tenean Beach 18, 128, 129, 140
Teresa, Vincent 64, 68, 110
Testa Building 83, 133, 135
Tham, Nam The 133
318 Lounge 105
Tim's Tavern 97
Tobin, Maurice 99
tongs 129, 131
Tong War 129, 131
Toothless Wah 133
Tortora, Carmen A. 66
*Town, The* 137, 141
Tran, Siny Van 133
Tran, Van 132
Treasury Departments 28
Tremont Street 27, 79, 101, 116
Triple O's bar 20, 85, 106, 119
Tse, Stephen 131, 132
Tucker, Sophie 76
Tulsa, Oklahoma 21, 55, 68, 69, 70, 120, 125, 126
Tyler Street 131, 132

**U**

*Underboss, The* 50, 63
United States Air Force 16
U.S. Attorney's Office 43
U.S. Court of Appeals 33, 120
U.S. District Court 24, 33, 43
U.S. Parole Commission 30

**V**

*Valhalla* 22
Vanzetti, Bartolomeo 38
Victory Road 40
Vietnamese 132, 133

**W**

Wahlberg, Mark 140
Wallace, Frank 38, 51, 81, 83, 133
Wallace, James 81
Wallace, Steve 9, 81, 84, 85
Walsh, Barney "Dodo" 9, 83, 133
Watertown 123
Weeks, John 85
Weeks, Kevin 11, 18, 22, 47, 85, 87, 88, 97, 106, 107, 119, 120
Weeks, Margaret 85
Welansky, Barnet "Barney" 81, 98, 99
Welansky, James 98, 99
Werner, Maurice 64
West Roxbury, Massachusets 70, 89
Wheeler, David 149
Wheeler, Roger 21, 42, 55, 70, 120, 125, 126
William J. Day Boulevard 96, 97
Winter Hill 21, 57, 68, 104, 120
Winter Hill Gang 11, 13, 18, 19, 20, 32, 34, 43, 45, 48, 53, 54, 55, 56, 58, 60, 66, 68, 72, 85, 87, 88, 90, 97, 102, 103, 104, 105, 120, 122, 125, 128
Winter, Howie 10, 11, 19, 20, 58, 60, 89, 111
Witness Protection Program 19, 37, 58, 72, 76
Wolf, Mark L. 43, 149
Worcester, Massachusetts 61
World Jai Alai 21, 42, 55, 70, 125
Wrinkled Skin Man 133

**Z**

Zannino, Ilario "Larry" 28, 65, 71, 90, 91, 92

# ABOUT THE AUTHORS

B everly Ford is a Boston-based journalist and author who has spent more than twenty years as a reporter and freelance writer for the *Boston Herald*, the *New York Daily News*, the *London Times*, the *London Mirror*, *Access Magazine*, *Bloomberg News* and other publications. She has written about mob murders and court trials involving several people profiled in this book. She currently works as a freelance investigative journalist for the New England Center for Investigative Journalism. She has ghostwritten two books, including a 1991 book on the Kennedy family, and also authored a book on domestic violence in 2001 for *Information*. She was among several reporters awarded the 1991 Associated Press Spot News Award for team coverage of a train accident and received awards in 1991 and 1995 for juvenile justice reporting from Parents of Murdered Children. She was also a guest panelist at a 2009 Neiman Foundation series at Harvard University and has lectured on crime and breaking news coverage at Boston-area colleges and universities.

S tephanie Schorow is a Boston-based freelance writer, author, teacher and artist. She is the author of *The Crime of the Century: How the Brink's Robbers Stole Millions and the Hearts of Boston*; *East of Boston: Notes from the Harbor Islands* (The History Press, 2008); *Boston on Fire: A History of Fires and Firefighting in Boston*; and *The Cocoanut Grove Fire*. She was the editor of *Boston's Fire Trail: A Walk Through the City's Fire and Firefighting History* (The History Press, 2007). She has spent thirty years working for various news organizations, including the *Boston Herald*, the *TAB* chain, the *Stamford Advocate* and the Associated Press. She currently works as a freelancer for the *Boston Globe* and teaches writing at the Cambridge Center for Adult Education. She is working on her next book, tentatively titled *Drinking Boston: A History of the City and Its Spirits*.

Visit us at
www.historypress.net